PRACTICING THE PRESENCE OF THE GODDESS

Author of

Goddess Meditations
A Woman's Book of Rituals & Celebrations

PRACTICING THE PRESENCE OF THE GODDESS

EVERYDAY
RITUALS
TO
TRANSFORM
YOUR WORLD

BARBARA ARDINGER, PH.D.

NEW WORLD LIBRARY
NOVATO, CALIFORNIA

New World Library
14 Pamaron Way
Novato, California 94949

Copyright © 2000 by Barbara Ardinger
Front cover design by Kathy Warinner
Text design and typography by Mary Ann Casler
Illustrations by Kathy Warinner

All rights reserved. This book may not be reproduced in whole or
in part, or transmitted in any form, without written permission from the
publisher, except by a reviewer who may quote brief passages
in a review; nor may any part of this book be reproduced, stored in
a retrieval system, or transmitted in any form or by any means
electronic, mechanical, photocopying, recording, or other,
without written permission from the publisher.

Library of Congress Cataloging-in-Publication Data

Ardinger, Barbara, 1941–
Practicing the presence of the goddess / by Barbara Ardinger.
p. cm.
Includes bibliographical references and index.
ISBN 1-57731-173-6 (alk. paper)
1. Goddess religion. I. Title.
BL473.5 .A73 2000
291.1'4—dc21   00-055893

First Printing, September 2000
ISBN 1-57731-173-6
Printed in Canada on acid-free paper
Distributed to the trade by Publishers Group West
10 9 8 7 6 5 4 3 2 1

First, as always, to my son Charles and, now, to his terrific girl friend, Phish. Charles is a poet, Phish is an artist. I love seeing how much in love they are and how their creativity blooms in astonishing ways.

Second, to my brother, Dale Rohne, and his partner, Tim Spaulding. In the spring of 1999, Dale was diagnosed with a nasty type of cancer, and all through the summer we wondered if he would live. As I begin writing this (November, 1999), however, there is good news: Dale has phoned to say the cancer is in remission. He has the love of his sister and his community to help with the healing.*

Third, to Munro Magruder, marketing and subsidiary rights director, and Georgia Hughes, editorial director, New World Library. When Georgia joined the staff of NWL early in 1999, Munro handed her a copy of *A Woman's Book of Rituals & Celebrations*. Georgia read the book, liked it, and phoned me. "We'd like you to rewrite the book," she said, "and we'll publish it in an elegant new edition." That's one of the best phone calls I've ever received.

---

* Although I ordered Dale to stay alive till the book was published, the cancer metastacized and he died on June 1, 2000.

Contents

Candle. Circle. Magic.	x
Foreword by Burleigh Mutén	xi
Preface	xiii
Introduction: Still Looking for an Equal-Opportunity Religion	xiv

PART 1
OUR MANY-SPLENDORED GODDESS — 1

Three Goddesses of Transformation — 1
- Serenissima, Goddess of Taking Care of Yourself — 2
- Bringing Serenissima into Your Life — 2
- Theadonna, Goddess of Gratitude — 5
- Sancta Chrona, Goddess of Living in the Now — 8

Our Many-Splendored Goddess — 10
- The Goddess of the Spheres — 11
- The First Sphere: The Goddess of the Cosmos and Ancient Days — 12
- A Ritual to Celebrate the Goddess of the Cosmos — 15
- The Second Sphere: The Triple Goddess — 16
- The Third Sphere: Mother Earth — 21
- The Innermost Sphere: The Dark Goddess — 25
- Beneath the Spheres: The Quantum Goddess — 27
- A Ritual to Celebrate the Goddess in Women — 27

PART 2
A VERY BRIEF HISTORY OF MODERN FEMINIST SPIRITUALITY — 31

Witches and Pagans and Druids — 31
- "I Am a Witch" — 33
- High-Church and Low-Church Witchery and the Goddess Stream — 35
- Covens and Circles — 37
- Green Spring Circle, a Fictitious Coven — 39
- Leadership and Hierarchy — 41
- Coming Home to the Goddess — 43
- A Ritual for the Path of My Faith — 44

PART 3
PRACTICING HER PRESENCE TODAY — 47

Worship — 47
Re-creating the Sacred Dimension — 48
- Deep Thought — 50
- A Ritual of Thoughtfulness — 50
- Good Works — 51
- A Ritual of Good Work — 52
- Experiential Play — 53
- A Ritual to Manipulate Reality — 54
- Devotion — 55
- A Ritual of Devotion — 55

Practicing Her Presence Every Day	58
A Ritual of Creativity	64
Craftella	68
Traditions	70
Ritual Practice	71
An Eclectic Full Moon Ritual	74
Creating Ritual	80
Purification	80
Casting the Circle	81
Stating the Intention	83
Raising Energy	84
Trance Work	86
Grounding Energy	87
Opening the Circle	88
Unencumbered Ritual	89

PART 4
TRANSFORMING YOUR WORLD

Transforming Your World	93
Magic	93
A Ritual of Personal Power	98
Our Altar — The Earth in Miniature	99
The Four Elements	102
Elemental Fire	103
Elemental Water	103
Elemental Air	104
Elemental Earth	104

Directions of the Elements	106
Altar Etiquette	108
Portable Altars	109
Magical Tools	110
Sword	111
Wand	112
Cup	112
Pentacle	112
Candles	113
Making Your Own Tools	114
Ritual Dress	114
Creating an Invocation	115
How to Talk to a Deity	118
The Blessed Bees	123
Three Rituals of Blessing	124
A Self-Blessing	124
A Blessing for Our Foremothers	128
A Blessing for Our Children	130
Appendix A: Revisionist History	134
Appendix B: Goddess 101 Basic Library	137
Acknowledgments	139
About the Author	141

Candle. Circle. Magic.

... so I'm just sitting here,
sitting through the year's dark night,
waiting, wondering, watching.
Is there anything I can do?

"Light a candle," someone tells me,
"Cast a circle. Let the magic begin."

So I light and cast and let.
And it's still, and it's dark,
and I'm wondering when the light will rise.

"Light your candle," Someone murmurs,
"Cast the circle of your need," She whispers,
"The magic is always in you," She says.

Again I light, again I cast, and I let it be,
and — o wonders arise — I'm still here,
working, playing, being in the world.

Her candle — that's always you and me,
Her circle — that's our blessed dreamlit world,
Her magic — that's you and me, community,
working, playing, being in the world ...

— Barbara Ardinger, Ph.D.
Winter Solstice, 1999

Foreword

Smiling is a sacred act. Singing *Ma* in the shower and manipulating my computer mouse are also sacred acts. The rustling leaves outside the window and the check I wrote to my favorite charity are sacred objects when I remember who I am — not just a woman or a daughter of the Goddess, but an embodiment of Her wisdom and loving kindness. Again and again, Barbara Ardinger brings us home to the goddess within ourselves and in all that surrounds us here on Earth.

With her ever present wit and wisdom, Barbara gifts us again and again as she shows us the numerous ways we can practice the presence of the Goddess in our daily lives as well as within formally defined saced space. Beyond personal rituals to bless and empower ourselves, she explains the modern feminist spirituality movement in a manner I have never seen so concisely presented. She explains the rudiments of altars, invocations, trance, grounding, the symbols, elements, and etiquette of ritual — all the time making it clear that we sacred women must listen to ourselves and be guided by our own divine wisdom to create what is meaningful to us in ceremony and in our lives.

Practicing the Presence of the Goddess is an offering for the novice, the solitary, and the Wiccan Priestess. By creating an imaginary coven called Spring Green Circle, Barbara makes it easy to understand the interpersonal dimension and the gathered power which is possible by practicing in a group. Her scholarship and friendly style of writing make her a true teacher, one whose power is so settled within herself that she is a catalyst, igniting the creative power of her reader. All practitioners of women's spirituality will find the wisdom of the Goddess, of Barbara, and of herself in this book.

Practicing the Presence of the Goddess closes with rituals to bless ourselves, our foremothers, and our children. In this way, Barbara draws us into the spiral of time, connecting the visible to the invisible. There, between the worlds, we weave a sacred tapestry, the web of women's wisdom. When you complete your first reading of *Practicing the Presence of the Goddess,* you are sure to find yourself full of light, glowing from your center, reminded to live with intention, reminded of who you are, a goddess with tools and insight to put to use. Get ready to receive your blessings!

Burleigh Mutén
author of *Return of the Great Goddess*
Amherst, Massachusetts
July 10, 2000

Preface

After Georgia Hughes phoned me, the first assignment I gave myself was to reread the two editions of *Rituals & Celebrations*. What did I write ten years ago? Five years ago? As I read, I sometimes said to myself, "Gee, this makes sense. The writing is still pretty good, too." Other times, however, it was, "Whoa — how naïve I was." Or, "I sure don't believe that anymore. Time to rewrite!"

Regarding the practice of the presence of the Goddess, my basic thinking has not changed. I believed then, and still believe today, in the inalterable fact that we dwell and dance the dance of our lives in the presence of the Goddess. In Her presence, every day, we sleep, awaken, go to work or school, do our recreational things, eat and digest and eliminate, make love, and go back to sleep. But we get so busy doing all these things that we often forget where we *really* are. Modern life makes it very difficult to remember the presence of the Goddess.

One day it happens, who knows how, that something makes us pay attention. Maybe the Goddess in one of Her manifestations causes something to "happen" that knocks us upside the head. However it happens, we become inspired to practice the presence of the Goddess. We begin to manifest Her positive feminine energy. Slowly and surely, we begin to create a life based on Her holy energy, on the principles She manifests. Incorporating Her presence — and please remember that "incorporate," from the Latin *corpus*, "body," means to *embody*. Today I believe more than ever in the indispensability of community. We must cherish each other and cherish our planet. I believe that it's never too late to start building community.

Introduction

Still Looking for an Equal-Opportunity Religion

Most of us were introduced to religion in a church or temple that looked pretty much like a courtroom. The spectators (us) were lined up in rows, and it was expected that we would pay attention, be on our best behavior, and not embarrass our parents. Between the front row of seated spectators and the place where the important people (mostly men) stood were an empty space and sometimes a wall or a fence whose purpose was to keep us plebians out of the high holy place. The officers of this church/court (mostly men) stood between us and the holy place, talking down to us like fathers addressing not-quite-well-behaved children. Although the judge was absent, we all knew he was a powerful and judgmental old man in a long robe. *He knew if we'd been good or bad.*

Many of us are no longer satisfied with this setup. We're tired of sin and guilt and bloody gods. We long for caring and nurturing and loving-kindness. We want open access to the divine, and we've figured out that the divine essence of the world manifests *as the world* — in people, in plants and animals, in rivers and canyons and plains. We understand that the divine can manifest in our cities and neighborhoods and communities. Many of us have read the books that explain how people used to worship a Mother Goddess who created the world and embodied the earth. We've read how people used to honor each other, how "thou shalt not kill" once really meant something. We've read books[1] that

---

1. Merlin Stone, *When God Was a Woman* (San Diego: Harcourt Brace Jovanovich, 1976). Elinor Gadon, *The Once & Future Goddess* (San Francisco: Harper & Row, 1989). Marija Gimbutas, *The Civilization of the Goddess: The World of Old Europe* (San Francisco: HarperSanFrancisco, 1992).

Introduction

describe the echoes and remains of the earliest religions that were all but erased from existence by the later desert-born religions. We've read what once might have been and wondered if it might be again.

Not only that, but every day we see with our own eyes what shape our planet is in: the polluted air and water, the strip-mined and dumped-on land, the burned and clear-cut forests, overdevelopment at the expense of every other creature on the planet. We see what overpopulation and ethnic jealousies are doing to our mother earth. If we're going to survive as individuals or as a planetary community, we need the living presence of the Goddess and all of Her children (even the ugly, unfriendly, and inanimate ones).

Intuitively, seriously, playfully, we've come to a new understanding of what our faith is about. We're creating an equal-opportunity religion. Based on images and figures found in caves and rubble and on hints found between the lines of the standard-brand holy books and dissertations, we're inventing our old-time religion. We're building modern versions of what might have been the archaic religion of the Great Goddess, who was, and still is, the Queen of Heaven, Earth, and the Underworld.

When we attend to the Goddess, therefore, we do it alone or with a few close friends. I originally wrote this book and its rituals to be used by a woman at her private altar in her private space. That is still its primary purpose. The little rituals are personal and unencumbered; they're mystical poetry intended to touch both heart and mind and help Everywoman practice the presence of the Goddess in her everyday life.

If you see yourself in any of the foregoing, this book is for you. You've come to a point where you want to acknowledge the change in our worldview and the change in our view of the divine. You agree that we can all find our proper places in the community of our blessed planet.

> ### A Note on Unencumbered Ritual
>
> "Unencumbered ritual" is a term I invented when I wrote *A Woman's Book of Rituals & Celebrations* in 1990 to describe ritual that does not require an elaborate setup — altar, magical tools, script, invocations, or robes. Reader, you need to be aware that the little poetic "rituals" scattered throughout this book are not necessarily entire rituals. If you are a solitary, you can use them as meditations. You can also set up a ritual circle, invoke elemental powers or goddesses, and use a poem as the center of the ritual. You can take a poem to your group and build a ritual around it. However you use the poems, use them with intention and with my love.

What This Book Is About

As the modern pagan community enters its fourth decade, it seems to me that we need to know where we stand and what we stand for. This book, therefore, goes back to the basics. Since the 1970s, when people began writing popular books about gods and goddesses, there have been a flood of definitions and a landslide of ambiguity. Who is the Goddess? Who are the people who call themselves pagans? Who are the people who call themselves Witches? Using a metaphor of a set of nesting spheres to explain who the Goddess is, the first half of the book sets forth my answers to these questions. Next, because our community is quite large, it seems appropriate to distinguish between what I call High-Church and Low-Church Witchery and the Goddess Stream. To show that the people who come together to practice the presence of the Goddess are regular, normal, everyday people, I create a fictitious coven whose rituals we will attend. Finally, I address the thorny issues of leadership and hierarchy.

The next part of the book is about practicing the presence of the Goddess. I begin with worship and the sacred dimension, which I see in

Introduction

four aspects. I also present a list of specific ways to practice Her presence — self-talk, chanting, making art, and other activities.

Worship of the Goddess — like worship of any deity — takes form in ritual. The next part of the book, therefore, sets forth generally accepted elements of ritual and explains how to create the kind of ritual I prefer, which I call "unencumbered ritual." Finally, I look at some of the specifics — the four elements, directions, altar etiquette, magical tools, ritual dress, invocations, and talking to deities.

This book opens and concludes with two sets of personal rituals that I invite you to use or adapt to your own personal practice of Her presence. Think of these rituals as bookends, if you will, or the boundaries of the sacred space that we create together as I write and you read this book.

What do you need to use this book? Not a lot, really. Here's your starter kit:

- Your intention, or the purpose for your ritual. Your intention can be personal growth and healing, help for your friends, healing for the earth and her creatures, or a celebration of a season or sabbat. As I see it, intention is the most important element of any ritual. You need to know what you're doing and why.
- Your active, fearless imagination.
- An hour or two of quiet time where you won't be disturbed by phone calls or kids or roommates wanting to know what on earth you're doing all alone in there.
- A table, shelf, or chest to use as the foundation for your altar.
- Goddess images, candles and holders, and such natural gifts as herbs, flowers, stones, and crystals.
- Cherished objects to help you remember and to serve as props for your sacred drama (which is one definition of ritual).

Please note that when I began writing books about the Goddess, I was much more interested in correspondences and props and tools than I am now. I believed that we needed symbols of everything on our altars. I believed that we needed things to most effectively practice Her presence.

Today I'm more relaxed, although, Goddess knows, my friends tell me that my home still looks like a metaphysical bookstore. But there's a significant difference between then and now. I still cherish my things, but these days I don't depend on them. I am finding, in fact, that although I enjoy ritual as much as ever and attend and help facilitate public rituals and lead private ones, when I'm alone I just don't do lots of rituals. I meditate. (Sometimes.) I pray. (Frequently.) I endeavor to be aware of Her presence and I give thanks. (Often.) What is inside manifests outside, and vice versa, but I no longer feel the need to depend on props to assist in the manifestation.

If you love things on your altar, however — go for it! Ours is a religion of beauty and pleasure and joy. Make your living space as beautiful as you can and enjoy it every day of your life.

Part 1

Our Many-Splendored Goddess

Three Goddesses of Transformation

Lately I have found myself much engaged with Found Goddesses. Found Goddesses[1] are the modern ones to whom we pray in situations never dreamt of by ancient peoples. Today, for example, we are Finding goddesses of computers and potluck, and I am, in fact, writing a book of Found Goddesses that includes goddesses of meetings, duct tape, air conditioning, apartment rental, and good hair cuts. We should, I believe, take the Goddess and our worship seriously, but we don't have to abandon our sense of humor when we practice the presence of the Goddess. Finding a goddess is an act of creativity. It's an act of noticing a need and meeting it. It's an act of practicing the presence of the Goddess Whose aspects may be both traditional and modern.

Reader, take some time now to interact with these Found Goddesses: Serenissima, Theadonna, and Sancta Chrona. Invite them into your life and allow them to help you change your life.

---

1. This wonderful phrase was created by Morgan Grey and Julia Penelope in *Found Goddesses: Asphalta to Viscera*, illustrated by Alison Bechdel, (Norwich, Vt.: New Victoria Publishers, 1988).

Serenissima, Goddess of Taking Care of Yourself

It was true for Grandma and for Mom and it's still true for us: woman's work is never done. With economic conditions being what they are for us ordinary folks, we are working harder than ever, often holding down two jobs or working excessive overtime, plus trying to do our share of housework and childcare. On top of working too hard, we try to spend some time with our children, our partners, and our parents, not to mention keeping in touch with our friends. Some days it's impossible to keep up. Some days we can't even cope.

It's time to get help. It's time to call on the Goddess Serenissima, She Who holds our hands, rubs our shoulders, tempts us into a bubble-bath, and teaches us the vital, life-preserving skills of self-love, self-care, and self-time.

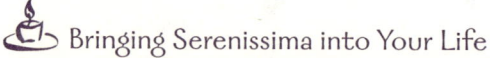 Bringing Serenissima into Your Life

This is a two-part ritual whose intention is to bring the power and beauty of Serenissima into your life and relief into your schedule. Your intention is to create a whole day of self-time two weeks or one month from now. You are, therefore, asking Serenissima to intervene in your life in all Her ordinary, magical ways to reschedule your obligations and clear a day on your calendar.

For Part 1 of the ritual, decorate your altar with beautiful things you love. Put a calendar page or the pages of your daily organizer covering the next thirty days, starting today, on the altar (but out of the way of candle flames and dripping wax). Invoke Serenissima with these words:

> Holy Goddess Serenissima,
> touch my life
> and give me the space and time
> to nourish myself

to cherish myself.
    Sovereign Serenissima
    touch my life.
    Show me the path to your peace.

Light the candles and visualize Her fingers moving across your organizer and making changes. See meetings being postponed, deadlines being rescheduled, the work being shared more equitably.

Understanding that Serenissima works in subtle ways, remain aware of possibilities during the next two weeks. Look for ways to facilitate the changes you invoked. You need to be alert. She may create the opportunities, but it's your own action that will open up your self-time.

One of the lessons Serenissima may give you may be to learn to say *no*. Practice saying this powerful little word at appropriate times. Another lesson may be to learn to set priorities and delegate tasks, both at work and at home. In very practical terms, this may mean that you should stop trying to do it all yourself. You may have to learn to give up perfectionism; sometimes good enough really is good enough.

Work with Serenissima. Let Her guide you. And when your promised day shows up, seize it.

Do Part 2 of the ritual during the morning of your day. *Your day*.

Settle the logistics the day before, if not earlier: who does what, when and where, and to whom while you're utterly unavailable. Tape notes for your family to every surface in the kitchen and bathroom if you have to. Tell them to do it themselves. Let them learn to be resourceful.

Decorate your room and your altar with your favorite colors. Spray your favorite scent into the air and open a new potpourri. Touch your favorite essential oil to your throat, wrists, and heart. Have your

most beautiful chalice ready, half filled with water. Speak to the Goddess:

> Most Serene Majestic Goddess,
> I thank You for this day.
> Tranquil One, o Easeful One,
> I thank You for all my days.
> Goddess of Harmony and Repose,
> I celebrate all days as Your days.

As you light your candles, imagine that each tiny flame is a star that brings serenity into your life.

> Beautiful and gracious Serenissima,
> Show me Your paths of peace,
> Show me Your ways of woven light and dark,
> Show me Your threads of shining work and play,
> and I will move with You,
> and in You I will dance.

Take a sip of water from your chalice. Savor the way the water touches your lips and tongue; savor its taste. Consider the natural, unthinking way your mouth accepts the water, the way you swallow without thinking how to do it.

Know that this sip of water is a tiny gift from the Goddess, a single drop of the essence of the Most Serene One. Remember also that water makes up over ninety percent of our human body and that water also carved out the Grand Canyon. Remember the simple power of water, that water flows around all obstacles. Feel the water's glowing, calming essence as it enters your body and remember that all nourishment — from your mother's milk to whatever you plan to have for lunch today — enters your body and your being and becomes your body and your being.

Continue to sip water from your chalice and recall what the chalice is. It's the true holy cup, the original Holy Grail. It's your Mother's breast.

Remember that as you accept Serenissima into your life, in sips and in seconds of time, She is always present. Like the water, She becomes part of you and you are thus gradually and imperceptibly transformed. As you move in the ways of Serenissima, you embody Her and become more serene.

We are all, each of us and all of us, drops of Her gentle rain on a parched and thirsty land, and when we bring Her serenity into our lives, one day at a time, we are bringing Her back to all of Her children.

Leave a few drops of water in the bottom of your chalice and treasure all these things and ponder them in your heart.

> Most Serene Majestic Goddess,
> I accept this day.
> Tranquil One, o Easeful One,
> I accept all my days.
> Goddess of Harmony and Repose,
> I accept all days as Your days.

Remembering that the circle is open but never broken, spend the rest of your day doing whatever you want to do.

Theadonna, Goddess of Gratitude

The name of this Found Goddess is constructed from the Latin words for *Goddess and gift*. Although our lives often become so busy we forget Her and fail to notice Her gifts, She never forgets us. She is ever generous.

Reader, slow down a minute and look around. Can you identify

Theadonna's gifts in your life? Some may arrive in disguise, in plain brown wrappers or delivered by strange messengers. We need to train ourselves to be able to recognize them. That training has two phases: mindfulness and gratitude.

Mindfulness is paying attention, being vigilant. Every time you catch yourself being unreasonably angry, sinking into self-pity, focusing only on the negative in a person or a situation, becoming fearful of some invisible (and probably imaginary) menace — stop it! Pay attention. Ask yourself what's really going on here. Take a deep breath. Recall Theadonna to your heart and mind. Look around and identify Her gifts to you.

For example, here's a list of five of Her gifts that I identify today:

1. My son, his girlfriend, my two cats, and I are all healthy.
2. They have a clean, safe place to live; the cats and I have a clean, safe place to live.
3. Publishers send me review copies of books. Some are books I want to read. I get to keep them. (My friends get most of the rest. The dregs go to a used bookstore.)
4. My plants are all green and healthy. Some of them are blooming.
5. I have a good car that starts every morning and is comfortable to drive.

"Well, big deal," I hear you say. "These are just ordinary, everyday things."

"You're right," I reply. "Ordinary things, indeed."

It's their very ordinariness that makes them wonderful. Every ordinary day is a blessing of the Goddess.

Take time to identify five ordinary, everyday things for which you are grateful today. Make a little ritual of your list-making by lighting a candle, playing music, talking to the Goddess.

1.
2.
3.
4.
5.

If it took you awhile to finish this little list, reflect on why this is so. Do you think you're in charge? Do you expect impossible things to happen just at your say-so? Big miracles, the kind sometimes promised by the gurus, are not the point here.

Theadonna is the Goddess of gratitude for the little things that keep our lives moving along, day by day. How often do you say please and thank you, even to store clerks and busboys? How often do you thank the flowers for blooming (they would, anyway) or your email for actually working or your videos for coming out of the VCR? When you push the button on the soda or snack machine and your selection is what you actually get, do you say thank you?

Invite Theadonna into your life. The way I keep Her beside me is to write in my gratitude journal every night before bed. Some days, yes, all I can think to write are that I'm still breathing in and out (on stressful days, this is a big deal to an asthmatic) and that I have a warm bed to sleep in or that no one yelled at me today. Some days are not great, but every single day has some gift in it. Some days the gifts are exceedingly small. Occasionally, however, they may be major miracles.

Here's a true story. For years, the left lens kept falling out of my glasses. It fell out while I was drumming; it fell out in my car; once it even fell out when I was standing in line at Disneyland. It got to the point where I was carrying a tiny screwdriver in my purse. One Monday last spring, I came home, took my glasses off, changed clothes, put my glasses back on, and walked into the living room. The lens fell out again. I heard it hit the floor. I got down on hands and knees and looked for it. As cats always do, Heisenberg helped me. We looked and looked, but that lens just wasn't there. Fortunately, I had spare glasses. On Tuesday, I phoned around to find a new optometrist, as my old one had retired a few years ago. The optometrist I found was — aha, it's a small world — a friend of my old one. I got my eye exam and ordered regular glasses and sunglasses. With nice frames and bifocals and tints and coatings, the price was nearly $400. Wednesday, I spent all day saying, "Goddess, I need $400 to pay for these glasses. I could take it out of savings, but that's rent money." Deciding not to worry, I just did my work. When I got home and opened the mail, there was a check for $500 from the publisher of *Goddess Meditations*. They'd sold the foreign rights.

A week later, Schroedinger, my calico cat, found the missing lens. It was under my bed. Now it's on my altar.

Whether all these things were coincidence or whether they were the actions of the Goddess in my life doesn't matter. I am grateful.

Reader, what is your story? How has the Goddess moved in your life? perhaps you can create an altar or ritual around your story.

Sancta Chrona, Goddess of Living in the Now

She is our Sacred Timekeeper, the One Who ticks off the seconds of our lives, the minutes, hours, days, weeks, months, and years that we live in but seldom ever notice.

How does time move? You already know the two theories. One asserts that time is linear. Each tick of time is like each letter of each word of each sentence in a book. We read one word at a time, one sentence at a time, always in the same direction (except for those perverse people who read the end of mystery novels first). It's very orderly: time past, time present, time future. Remember, however, that there's a reason they call it "verb *tense*." Living a linear life and focusing all the time on the past and the future are not always healthy ways to live.

Sancta Chrona reminds us that there's another way to look at

Our Many-Splendored Goddess

time. Time is Now. It is always Now, and Now is always cycling, always spiraling, ever turning and returning. It is always Now, because the past and the future are mental constructs. Right this minute, they're not real. When the past was real, it was Now. When the future becomes real, it will be Now.

But you know that. I'm just reminding you.

Serenissima, Theadonna, and Sancta Chrona are sister Goddesses. First, they advise us to take better care of ourselves. Second, they tell us to become vigilant. We must pay attention to the gifts of the Goddess and give thanks for them. Third, they remind us that it's time to give up regretting lousy things we once did and continually basking in good things we once did. Now is the time to stop worrying about future disasters or anticipating things that may never come to pass.[2]

Now is real. It's all we've got.

Living in the now goes with being grateful. Listing things for which we're grateful helps us focus our mind on where we are right now. When I'm feeling anxious (and that's something I'm quite good at), therefore, I make another list. Here's my Right This Minute list:

1. Right this minute, there's food in the refrigerator.
2. Right this minute, there's catfood in the cabinet.
3. Right this minute, there are clothes in the closet.
4. Right this minute, there are books on the shelves.
5. Right this minute, there's money in the bank.

Basics again. But I'm not defensive about seeing basics. Basic things keep me from worrying. Basic things keep me living in the Now. Like Her Sisters, Sancta Chrona is a Goddess of basic things.

Stop reading and make your own Right This Minute list. Make a little ritual if you like. Light a candle; play music.

---

2. You understand, of course, that we live in both kinds of time. It is prudent to keep our insurance paid up, to apologize for gaffes and other mistakes, to make plans for tomorrow and beyond, and to keep our promises.

1.

2.

3.

4.

5.

If you want to, create rituals around the goddesses or around your lists. A ritual of gratitude is always good, and rituals honoring basic, ordinary things keep our spirituality rooted right where it should be: here on our beautiful living earth.

Our Many-Splendored Goddess

When we decide to practice the presence of the Goddess, who are we talking about and just what on earth do we imagine we're going to do? How are we going to spend our days, our nights? Will our life change, or what? When we create and enact a ritual, what kinds of energies are we invoking? What is their source? What is the return on our investment of thought, work, experience, and devotion?

When we declare that the Goddess is the source of our being and our energy, these are vital questions, for we're changing our lives. We're dreaming up an ancient deity and reinventing a religion. We're creating a spirit-affirming way of life, not returning to the Neolithic, but bringing its peace and creativity to our modern world. We're singing the Goddess into our lives. We're dancing the Goddess out of Her five-thousand-year eclipse.

Her essence is many-splendored and many-layered. It's complex and simple, abstract and concrete, spiritual and earthy, superhuman and human, transcendent and immanent — all at the same time. Examining the Goddess is like trying to get a soap bubble under a microscope. When we try to describe Her many-layered essence, therefore, we find ourselves taking refuge in paradox and extravagant language. That's because we're trying to explain the inexplicable, and words can get us only halfway there.

I find that it is figurative language that most successfully describes the holistic concept we call "Goddess." When we talk about the Goddess of Ten Thousand Names, therefore, we may say she is like our physical mother or like falling rain returning to the ocean (similes). We can think of Her as the feminine principle (metonymy, in which a part stands for the whole), or we can see Her as the earth (both personification and metaphor). When we talk about Goddesses, we often use metaphor: She is the moon (and Her names are Ix Chel and Levanah), She is love (Radha and Freya), She is creation (Spider Grandmother and Ishtar).

But what do we mean when we speak in figurative language? As well as we can, in our halting, stumbling way, we're stating our belief in an immanent, omnipresent Goddess.

The Goddess of the Spheres

To clarify my ideas about the Goddess, I turn to the most successful metaphor I can actually get my hands on, which is a set of wooden spheres. You've seen them in gift shops and catalogs: three, four, or five painted spheres, all nested one inside another. I have three or four sets of these spheres, one of which is actually egg-shaped, plus a couple of orphan spheres.

The outermost sphere is generally painted midnight blue and "is" (represents) the universe. On one of my sets, the heavenly constellations are painted in gold and the astrological sun sign symbols are red. The universe is the biggest, most abstract thing we think we can know; it's the big picture. And here we are, holding it in the palm of one hand.

Split the painted universe along its equator, open it up, and discover its contents. The solar system lies nested tidily inside. In one of my sets, the solar system is deep blue-green, and the planets are circular splotches of color.

Open the solar system and the sun emerges, mirror halves with two painted faces and matching sets of golden rays. In another set the third sphere is not the sun but a two-inch earth, its oceans and continents apparently taken from Renaissance maps, with Latin names and vast empty space to designate territories unexplored by Europeans: *Here Be Monsters.*

The innermost sphere is usually the moon, with two graceful painted faces and silver rays. In my egg-shaped set of five spheres (the insides of which are painted dark blue with gold stars), however, the innermost sphere is a fiery red and gold egg, complete with a tiny phoenix rising from the painted flames. In any set, the smallest sphere is the only one that's solid, the only one that doesn't contain and conceal yet another visible level of the cosmos. (Unless, of course, we include the atomic and subatomic levels of reality, in which case we can start all over again.)

If, as many of us believe or intuitively know, the Goddess "is" the cosmos, let's use our little set of painted spheres to discover Her layers.

The First Sphere: The Goddess of the Cosmos and Ancient Days

As the outermost sphere represents the Goddess, then, it shows Her universality, how She is the cosmos itself, the wholeness of creation. In the archaic creation myths, is it not the Goddess who gives birth to the stars, the suns, the moons, the planets and everything living on them? She forms everything out of Her own body and its fluids. She dances or sings or spins or weaves or shapes all things into being. In Her image are we made of clay, star stuff, pure energy. The Goddess is the Cosmic Mother; She's the mother of the cosmos.

We can accept this as literal truth or we can understand it as figurative language; to those with faith, it makes no difference. Like the myths presented in the first and second chapters of Genesis, any creation story is a record of faith because no reporter was there to witness and report it. The main differences between the creation myths of the standard-brand religions and the Goddess religions, of course, are the emphasis on spiritual creation and the illusory nature of matter in the former and the reality of matter and mud in the latter.

If there's a human culture in which the grandmother goddesses aren't ages older than the upstart warrior gods, it hasn't been unearthed yet. Goddesses were worshipped in Canaan long before the Hebrew tribes walked in, the sister-wives of Abraham and his sons and grandsons may have been priestesses of the indigenous Goddess religions, and goddesses were worshipped in the temple in Jerusalem from before the time of Solomon all the way up to the Babylonian Captivity. And before there was Allah, there was Al-Lat, whose name means simply "goddess." One of a trinity of desert goddesses named in the Koran, She was the All-Powerful One, worshipped by Mohammed's tribesmen, the Koreshites, as a giant uncut rock of white granite, which, it is said, is now hidden under the black curtains of the Kaaba in Mecca. The priests of the Kaaba are, in fact, still known as the Sons of the Old Woman.[3]

Here is a concrete way to look at the Ages of the Goddess. One of my teaching tools is a long paper timeline whose centuries are marked off in inches. On this timeline, the Protestant Reformation (1517 C.E.) is five inches from the present. The arrival of Buddhism in Tibet and the flight of the Prophet Mohammed from Mecca to Medina are fourteen inches back. The life of Jesus of Nazareth is twenty inches back, the arrival of Cybele in Rome two inches further back, the lives of Confucius, the Buddha, and Lao-Tsu (all of whom lived about 500 B.C.E.) another

---

3. For an extraordinary close reading of Genesis, see Savina J. Teubal, *Sarah the Priestess: The First Matriarch of Genesis* (Athens, Ohio: Ohio University Press/Swallow Press Books, 1984). For Al-Lat, see Patricia Monaghan, *New Book of Goddesses & Heroines* (St. Paul, Minn.: Llewellyn, 1997), p. 41, and Barbara Walker, *Women's Encyclopedia of Myths & Secrets* (New York: Harper & Row, 1983), p. 487.

three inches back. The Exodus and the Trojan War are both at about thirty-two inches. The Rig Veda was composed about 1700 B.C.E. (thirty-seven inches). Abraham, father of the standard-brand religions and said by them to be the first man to talk to God, lived around 1900 B.C.E., (thirty-nine inches from the present). Stonehenge I is four feet two inches back, Avebury and the Malta temple complex (ca. 4000 B.C.E.) are at about five feet, and Catal Huyuk (ca. 8000 B.C.E.) is another forty inches back. The Neolithic ends about twelve feet from the present. At one inch per century, the Willendorf Goddess is more than thirty feet from the beginning of the timeline. When I lay it on the floor, the timeline extends from the middle of my kitchen, through my dining room and living room, almost to my front door. The Acheulian Goddess, a female figure found in the Near East, is now housed in the Hebrew University of Jerusalem's Institute of Archaeology. How old is She? They date her to between 800,000 and 230,000 B.C.E. If I were to add the age of the Acheulian Goddess to my timeline, it would stretch out into the street.

Wrap your mind around that. Make your own timeline. Look up dates of events you are interested in and write them on it. You'll get a whole new outlook on history and so-called prehistory.

The ancient goddesses were cosmic grandmothers, and since we have names and artifacts of goddesses from all the lands of earth, we can say that, at least in this terrestrial sense, She is universal.

Her universality has led to diversification. That is, if there's a human activity, there's a goddess to sponsor, oversee, and protect it, from birth to death, before and beyond. There are goddesses of healing, wealth, scholarship, arts and crafts, manufacture, law and justice, history and poetry, domesticity, and war.

There are goddesses of the sun, moon, sky and stars, of weather, of night and day, of the four directions, of the four elements and the seasons, of time itself. There are goddesses of plantlife in general and plants in particular, likewise of the animal world and terrestrial features like mountains and springs.

There are creator goddesses, magical goddesses and shape-shifters, goddesses of all the aspects of love, ancestor goddesses and wise women, even one or two sewer goddesses.

 A Ritual to Celebrate the Goddess of the Cosmos

Take some time now to do the following ritual to celebrate the cosmic Goddess. You'll need something that represents the cosmos to you: your own set of nested spheres, a tektite or a meteorite, an egg or a seed, a star globe or a telescope. Think big (really big) and do this ritual outdoors if you can, in the quietest place you can find. Hold your symbol of the cosmos in both hands at your navel.

Read the following words or tape them beforehand and listen to them or use them as a model to write your own words.

> She is the cosmos itself, the womb of starry seas,
> for She contains all things and bears all things.
> Inspiring and expiring, She breathes,
> dancing on the golden solar wind,
> broadcasting her star stuff —
>
> She is the black hole and the kitchen pantry.
> She is the heartbeat of labor and love.
> She is the space between the stars and atoms.
>
> She is.
> She simply is,
> She is whatever is,
> She is What She Is,
> She Is.
>
> And I am part of Her.
> I Am.

Close your eyes, take several deep, easy breaths, and imagine your cosmic symbol expanding. See and feel it grow so big it holds you in its hands at its navel. See and feel it grow so immeasurably big that you are a speck floating inside it. Now look back at your own body and see it begin to whirl and twirl, to shine and sparkle. Watch your shining, swirling self grow and grow and grow. Inhale the scent of sweet, clean solar wind, hear the sounds of thunder and the hatching of an egg, listen to the beat of a baby's rattle and the roar of the tides. See yourself grow and glow until you fill the darkness of the cosmos, until you envelop and become its emptiness, its vastness, its darkness, and its light. Dark and light are in balance now, you and the cosmos are in balance, and now the balance explodes into a fountain of rainbow fireworks, a waterfall of words and sounds, a volcanic dance of living ... and then, here you are again, plain old ordinary regular you, the best beloved child of the cosmos.

When you're ready, open your eyes and spend as much time as you want examining your cosmic symbol, the earth beneath you, the sky above you.

The Goddess is at the same time both the cosmic creator and the created cosmos. She brings all things, visible and invisible, into existence, perhaps at the famous Big Bang or, more likely, in every instant of every day of every millennium. She destroys and recycles all that She creates, including Herself. We are part of Her cosmic, universal body, we are Her thoughts made flesh. We are Her songs, Her artwork, Her psychological projection. We are Her babies.

The Second Sphere: The Triple Goddess

The second sphere of our little painted set represents the solar system. It's our own neighborhood, our home, then the heart of a home is the mother. Let's use the second layer of our metaphor, there-

Our Many-Splendored Goddess

fore, to consider the Mother Goddess and Her two other aspects, the Maiden and the Crone. Together, Maiden, Mother, and Crone are the ancient Triple Goddess, which is the elder trinity. This is the trinity that represents the major stages of life itself as well as the stages of a woman's life.

Ever since the Greek dramatist Aeschylus made Athena say that a mother is just a sort of holding tank and hatchery for a man's sperm, making the father the real and only parent, mothers have been getting a bad rap. No matter what her failings, however, our mother is our door into this world. It was through her body that we came back to earth for another opportunity to work and play. That is surely worth honor and celebration.

To a baby, her mother (or grandmother, aunt, nurse, daycare teacher or aide, elementary school teacher, Brownie or Campfire leader) is her first goddess. To an infant, the woman who feeds and changes her, who keeps her warm and comfortable is, in fact, the whole world. To bigger, more independent kids, Mommy is still the main source of comfort and nourishment.

As our mother is in some way our own original goddess, so were humankind's original goddesses their mothers and grandmothers. Perhaps they were the literal mothers and grandmothers of the clans and tribes, perhaps they were the tough old women who did the healing, counseling, and judging, the ones who knew where to find food, how to build shelters, how to make useful things. Their power grew with the stories told about them until they took on superhuman dimensions and people eventually began to address prayers and petitions to them.

The oldest human figures are the Neolithic mothers — the fat, fecund Ladies of Willendorf and Laussel. They're perhaps the original earth mothers, and they represent the female principle of creating, procreating, mothering, nourishing, comforting, bringing rain, making the animals plentiful, both shining down and pushing up to make the crops grow. Although the people who carved and molded these figures of women with wide hips, generous stomachs, and pendulous breasts are officially termed "prehistoric" and "primitive," they were in fact highly civilized and had long-lived oral and artistic traditions and a symbolic "language of the Goddess."

Reproductions of the Willendorf Mother and the other Ur-Mothers are available from many sources, and I think it's helpful for us modern people to own at least one. You may also learn something about creation by making your own earth mama from clay, acrylic modeling compound, or mud.

Broadly speaking, there seem to be at least three kinds of mother goddesses:

- The queen mother, like Hera and Inanna, who may or may not actually bear children but who is sexual and fertile
- The good mother, like Demeter, Isis, and Mary, who is nearly always associated in myth or art with her daughter or son
- The terrible mother, like Kali and the grim, wicked stepmothers of all the fairy tales

We need to be careful, however, not to let our thinking get boobytrapped by the modern scientific processes of separation and classification. If we divide and subdivide and pigeonhole the mother goddesses, we end up with a multitude of trivialized mommies that pack none of the old power. We need to hold and contemplate a Willendorf Mother to rediscover what our old power may have felt like.

The holistic essence of the mother goddess is that *She is fertile*. She bears children and raises them, giving rewards and punishments as deserved. And she may not have only physical offspring; she can be the mother of art, music, literature, technology, discovery, industry, culture, charity, business, and anything else we can think of.

The youthful aspect of the Triple Goddess is the Mother's Daughter. Also called the Maiden or the Virgin, she is often portrayed as a little girl. She is pre-fertile, but she's fertile in her own way — as potentiality. Put it this way: the Maiden is the seed to her Mother's flower and her grandmother Crone's fruit.

The Maiden can represent the time of our life before we assume our adult responsibilities. She is beginnings, wildness, the wilderness. She is untouched. She is the young girl before menarche, as the Mother menstruates every month, and the post-menopausal Crone retains her "wise blood" to bear not children but power.

The Virgin aspect can also be hard to pin down. Although sometimes she's a virgin in the physical sense, the word "virgin" refers to more than sexual chastity and the intactness of the hymen. Its true meaning is independence, self-determination, freedom from external ownership and control. In this sense, it's possible for a Crone to be a Virgin, and, indeed, as the wheel of existence turns and life recycles, the Crone is reborn with the springtime as the Virgin.

The Maiden is elusive. Kore is the young daughter of Demeter, drawn by love from the meadow to the Underworld.[4] After Her marriage to Hades/Plouton, Kore, renamed Persephone, becomes the awesome Queen of the Underworld. Artemis (Diana) is the huntress, untouched by human (at least male) hands. She's also the matron of childbirth (a maternal duty), the Queen of Heaven and Witches (whence Dianic Wicca), and her many-breasted statue in Ephesus was one of the Wonders of the Ancient World. Are these all the same Artemis? Yes, they are; they show the all-encompassing generative power of the eldest goddess *Who was* from time out of mind and *Who was* before names were given.

---

4. See Jennifer Reif, *Mysteries of Demeter: Rebirth of the Pagan Way* (York Beach, Maine: Samuel Weiser, 1999), for a telling of the story without the infamous rape and for rituals to celebrate the Great Mother and Her Daughter.

Persephone and Artemis are examples not only of the diversity of the Goddess but also of the need to keep a holistic picture in mind when we talk about the Goddess. We can focus on specific aspects or goddesses for specific rituals, but realism (whatever that is) demands that we remember that *She is not to be fragmented or made frivolous.*

The Crone is the scariest aspect of the Triple Goddess, at least to men and in modern times when all women are desired to be forever age 19, size 2. If the Maiden is the daughter, the Crone is the grandmother, and occasionally the chaperone and baby-sitter. She's the old woman, and She's usually a widow, so She's the Virgin all over again. Because She destroys life so it can be recycled, She is sometimes called the Terrible Mother. She is the Dark Mother and She is Grandmother Death, and one of Her names is Hel. She's all the ugly old ones that bring justice and nightmares and doom. She's the Halloween witch. She's the Grandmother of God.

We're all going to grow old. Sooner or later, we'll all be Crones. We need, therefore, to consider the powers we can regain and use. We can have the wisdom based on the learning and experience of a long life; we can always learn a little more. We can find new ways to solve "mankind's" problems. The Crone may be our only hope.

The Triple Goddess is the center point of our neighborhood. She's the little girl, a tomboy on her bike or up in a tree, a child-mother taking over the care of her siblings, a teenager in school, at the mall, or out on the streets. She's the grown woman, working hard at home or in an office or plant, most likely doing two or more jobs and trying to raise her kids right and contribute something to the world in her spare time. She's the old woman — a widow in a retirement home or the neighborhood busybody keeping an eye on everything and expressing her opinions on it all. The Triple Goddess has charge of our everyday lives.

Although I still like this description of the Triple Goddess (that I wrote ten years ago), during the past decade I have begun to wonder if this configuration is sufficient to describe the lives of the women I know. Until the late twentieth century, most women did not survive to become Crones.[5] They died young, worn-out from too much childbearing and manual labor, from too little rest and nutrition. Today, as we live longer, we're coming to realize that women who used to be "old" are now "of a certain age." For several years, therefore, it has seemed to me that we need something between Mother and Crone. One of my friends uses the term "Queen." The Queen is the Mother whose children have grown up. While she's an empty-nester, she's hardly ready to retire. She still has enormous energy and she's got a lot to do. (Most of it seems to be questioning authority and raising hell.)

Elizabeth Davis and Carol Leonard have also addressed this issue, and their solution is to identify four seasons of life — Innocence, Nurturing, Power, and Wisdom — each of which contains a trinity of aspects: Initiation, Integration, and Transformation. These seasons and stages make a circle, which they call the women's wheel of life. Here we find not three but twelve stages: Daughter, Maiden, Blood Sister, Lover, Mother, Midwife, Amazon, Matriarch, Priestess, Sorceress, Crone, and Dark Mother. The thirteenth stage — Transformer — ties them all together.[6]

The Third Sphere: Mother Earth

The third sphere in one of our little nested sets is the sun. In our metaphor, this little painted sun can speak to us of warmth, nourishment, heat, and growth. It can remind us that the sun (and what it stands for: positive, projective energy, intellect, light) is not inevitably

---

5. And so our popular "croning" ritual is a modern invention. In the olden days they saw no need, and never heard of, such an occasion.

6. Elizabeth Davis and Carol Leonard, *The Women's Wheel of Life: Thirteen Archetypes of Woman at Her Fullest Power* (New York: Viking Arkana, 1996). This book needs to be read by everyone still stuck in the Triple Goddess paradigm.

masculine, that women are smart and powerful and hot. It can also remind us that we know four-dozen goddesses of the sun, from the Japanese Amaterasu and the Baltic Saule to the Cherokee Unelanuhi and Rome's Juno Lucina. Most of the sun goddesses are older than Apollo (who was once a Mouse God), and it's also true that there are numerous moon gods, including Sin, upon whose holy mountain the Ten Commandments were carved into stone.[7]

Our little sun can thus nudge us past that tired cliché that confines women to lunar (reflective) energy and men to solar (projective) energy. It's time, in fact, to question not only "their" but also our own received wisdom. In creating modern feminist spirituality we created our own myths ("*herstory*") to counterbalance their "*history*." Twenty-five years later, perhaps we can put our elementary stories in their proper place and act like a grown-up religion.

In other sets of spheres, the third sphere is the planet earth, and this is my primary emphasis here: the earthiness of the Goddess. A few earth scientists and the earth-based religions tell us that the earth is really a living organism.[8] Her name is Gaia, which is a variant of the old Greek name for earth, *Ge,* from which we also get *geography, geology,* and the other earthwords. Gaia, the planet, is a sentient being. The rocks and mountains are her skeleton (although some mountains, like the Paps of Anu in Ireland, are her breasts), the oceans and rivers are her blood, green plants and the atmosphere are her respiratory system, either people or whales and dolphins are her brain and nervous

---

7. See Janet McCrickard, *Eclipse of the Sun: An Investigation into Sun and Moon Myths* (Glastonbury, UK: Gothic Image Publications, 1990) and Patricia Monaghan, *O Mother Sun! A New View of the Cosmic Feminine* (Freedom, Calif.: Crossing Press, 1994).

8. See Tim (Oberon) Zell, "Theagenesis: The Birth of the Goddess," delivered as a lecture, September 1970; reprinted in *The Witches Broomstick* (Feb. 1972); excerpted in L.L. Martello's *Witchcraft, the Old Religion* (1973); and reprinted with annotations in *Green Egg* (May 1988). Zell's thesis predates the popular Gaia Hypothesis formulated by James Lovelock and Lynn Margulis. Eight hundred years earlier, Hildegard of Bingen saw nature as alive and everything on earth as connected.

system, and caves are her vagina and womb. We have evidence of the womblike nature of sacred caves all over the world.

Gaia used to be able to take care of herself, adjusting her respiratory rate and temperature, for example, to bring herself back into balance in spite of her children's activities. She could keep herself clean. With the indignities and overwhelming greed of the Industrial Revolution and mankind that made it, however, she's been under constant attack. She suffers from being paved over, deep-mined and strip-mined, having bombs exploded inside her body, having her forests burned and clear-cut, and from every kind of pollution people can create. Do droughts and poisoned oceans show us that she's getting weaker? Do earthquakes, volcanic eruptions, and famine indicate that she's fighting back? Will she at last become so disgusted that she shrugs us off and starts all over again with new species?

Whether we take it literally or consider it to be a beautiful metaphor, the Gaia Thesis leads to ecofeminism,[9] which asserts that as the planet is sacred per se, so are all things living in and on it/her sacred, from mud to mountain peaks and from moose to mosquitoes. In practice, this means honoring so-called "primitive" and foreign people and not developing (i.e., destroying) their homelands. It means working actively to make sure everyone has a place to live and enough to eat every day. It means understanding that corporate culture often values profit over any human value. It means living a kinder life, shopping cautiously, not wasting resources and energy, and recycling, repairing, and reusing. Ecofeminism can lead to changes in life on earth — a change from the usual emphasis on having power over other people and animals and plants and the ground to sharing power with them — moving from dominion over the earth to partnership with it. It can mean thinking and

---

9. Still worth reading is Susan Griffin's incredibly touching prose poem, *Woman and Nature: The Roaring Inside Her* (New York: Harper & Row Perennial Library, 1978).

living not in power-over hierarchies but in equal-opportunity circles.

Who is likely to initiate and work hardest to carry through such a revolution? You can bet it's not the haves and the wannabes. The revolutionaries are the intelligent women and men who bring the Goddess down from being an abstract concept into real, live action. *That's us.*

The third sphere, our little painted earth, also represents the diversity and pluralism of our goddesses. The standard-brand religions are ferociously monotheistic: Thou shalt have no other gods — and especially no goddesses — except Me. Notice, however, that the First Commandment does not say, "there are no other gods but me." It says, "Don't worship them. Worship no one but me."

Some Goddess worshippers are also monotheistic: there's one titanic Goddess, and although She may have ten thousand names, She is unitary and unified. Some of us are pantheistic: the Goddess or goddesses or both manifest everywhere and in everything, which makes everywhere and everything holy, individually and collectively. Some of us are polytheistic: there really are all those goddesses, and they're important not only to the elder cultures that named them but also to us modern societies. Yes, aspects and duties of the goddesses overlap, so we know forty or fifty moon goddesses, three-dozen goddesses of beauty, and goddesses with names from A to Z. Not only that — we have a multitude of gods, too, all with their own names, attributes and associations, duties, and characters.

No matter what kind of ritual or spell we want to do, no matter what kind of energy we want to embody or stir into action, there's an appropriate goddess or god to invoke. Like the words in the thesaurus, however, the multitudinous deities may be similar but none is precisely synonymous with any other. That's part of the joy of a way of life in the Goddess or goddesses — we have so much to play with, so many energies to work with, so much to explore.

At the same time, however, we need to consider the issue of

cultural imperialism (which is really piracy). Like mainstream metaphysicians, we are great borrowers. But how do the people whose goddesses and gods we borrow feel about it? There have been loud and unresolved discussions (well, arguments) about WASP women setting up altars to African, Native American, and Asian goddesses or proclaiming themselves priestesses of goddesses whose traditions don't even have priestesses. "But the Goddess is universal," they protest, or, "we're entitled." Oh yeah? Of what does our entitlement consist?

This is not an easily resolvable issue. What I urge are caution and courtesy. If you're drawn to a goddess of different ethnicity than yours, examine your feelings carefully, do painstaking research, and approach Her and Her people with enormous respect. If they tell you to stop it and go away, do so. "But I mean well" is a lame excuse for cultural piracy.

The Innermost Sphere: The Dark Goddess

The innermost sphere of our nested set is sometimes the moon, sometimes the center of the earth. I see this center as both the fiery core of our planet and as the darkness under the ground. It's a dark fire. It's the darkness inside a seed or an egg, where something is germinating, waiting to be born. It's also the darkness of a warm bed where we get a good night's sleep and the grave where we dissolve into an elemental presence and wait for rebirth. Many ancient burial sites, in fact, reveal people curled up in fetal positions and painted with red ochre, which symbolizes menstrual blood.

At Her most basic, most elemental level, the Goddess is dark. She is black fire (another metaphor), a concrete abstraction, the bright light of the dark moon. It is time therefore to reconsider the darkness, the old dark ones, the old dark ways. Our society fears and is thus prejudiced against darkness. We need to balance light and dark, spirit and earth, male and female. We need to remember the forgotten old ones, the forgotten histories.

It is the result of five thousand or more years of persistent racism and sexism, plus a long tradition of scholarly racism that makes us believe that the white male is the norm in all things. As far as we know, humankind first arose in Africa (long called the "Dark Continent") to walk on two feet and create civilization. All the earliest peoples were small and dark. It is racism that makes us think the tall blond people are the founders of civilization, when actually they wiped out (or married) the people who had lived in the lands they now occupy. Much of what we know as occult wisdom and magic was being written at the time the countries of Western Europe were creating their empires. Soldiers, explorers, and gentleman archaeologists plundered the rest of the world, stealing statues and other artifacts and bringing them home to put in museums. That these items were sacred meant nothing; they were trophies. Ruling the native people became the "white man's burden."

It is racism that made the dichotomies of white = good / black = bad, or spirit = light = good / earth = flesh = darkness = the devil = bad. Wrapping things or people in white light to purify and protect them is racist, sexist, and imperialist.

My goddess is the cosmic mother who enfolds and embodies the universe, the ordinary woman, and the quiet dark fire at the center of the holy planet we live on — all at the same time. In one of my novels, I describe Her:

> *She stood before them, as tall and deep and black as boundless space, as calm and wise and dark as the fertile earth. Her skin shone with purple and green and golden lights. She wore a crescent moon upon Her forehead, or perhaps it was two horns around which Her hair seemed to writhe. Around Her broad, muscular body lay the double helix of two vast serpents, their heads resting just above Her full breasts.... They saw the stars in Her skin.*

Reader, I have actually seen this goddess. In 1992, when I suffered a severe asthma attack and was rushed to the emergency room by two of my circle sisters, I lost consciousness at the door and was "gone" for twenty minutes. She was with me then. Although I later created a collage in which I tried to illustrate Her, it hardly comes close. Nor do my feeble words adequately describe Her.

Beneath the Spheres: The Quantum Goddess

And, finally, there's one last layer of the Goddess, the one that slips right through metaphors. Some call her Eris and make her the "patron saint" of chaos theory. I call her the Goddess Gotcha. Gotcha is one of my Found Goddesses, and Her kid brother is Coyote the Trickster. Gotcha has the strong sense of humor we all need to survive in this ridiculous civilization, and she has scant patience with pomposity and pride. She's the one who sends the cats in with their jingle toys when you're doing a high, holy ritual and everyone's taking themselves entirely too seriously. Gotcha makes you have to light a candle three times before it stays lit. She makes you tongue-tangled when your invocation goes on too long, and she plants puns and double-entendres in your reading and typos in your writing. The only thing to do when she appears is to greet her: *Hail, Gotcha, Fulla Fun and Outa Sight.*

A Ritual to Celebrate the Goddess in Women

For this ritual, you need your usual private space and something to make noise with — a doumbek or frame drum, a rattle, two sticks you can beat together, or your own hands to clap. Beat or clap as long as you want to whenever you come to the cue [Sound].

Before you begin the chant, imagine a bright, pulsing stream of spring-green light moving in a clockwise direction around your body. See and feel it start in the area of your heart and just let it go round and round for a few minutes. Don't force the light, and don't hurry this part of the ritual.

After a few minutes, let the light become strong enough to make you sway in tiny circles with it. When this circling is well established, turn the light into a green helix that spirals around your whole body, round and round from the top of your head to the base of your spine (if you're sitting) or your heels (if you're standing). Really feel this energy, feel its warmth and strength, let your body sway in its wind. Take as long as necessary to get the helix established so it can run on automatic while you do the chant. (If you're new at this, yes, it is real energy and, yes, it will keep going while you concentrate on the words.)

Read the following words or record them beforehand and listen to them or use them as a pattern to make up your own words. Women should say *I am* and men should say *She is* (or whatever the appropriate verb is) throughout this chant.

> I am/She is the powerful one. [Sound]
> I can do whatever must be done. [Sound]
>
> I can create new life. [Sound]
> Through my body, under my heart
> children come to earth, people come to life. [Sound]
> Through my mind, because of my will
> ideas come to life, material takes new form. [Sound]
> I can do whatever must be done. [Sound]
>
> I can build and I can tame
> I can plant and I can tend. [Sound]
> I am powerful
> I can do whatever must be done. [Sound]
> I can go forward and I can resist
> I can caress and I can be angry. [Sound]
> I am powerful
> I can do whatever must be done. [Sound]

I can nourish and I can punish
I can preserve and I can celebrate. [Sound]
I am powerful
I can do whatever must be done. [Sound]

I am the darkness and the light
I am the word and the dance
I am the growth and the harvest. [Sound]
I am power
I will do whatever must be done. [Sound]

At the end of the chant, make as much sound as you can. You can also repeat lines of the chant that you want to hear coming from your mouth again.

When the energy gets as strong as you want it to, direct the sounds into the spiraling green light, and then direct the light into your spine. Let it move up and down your spine for about one minute, then take several deep breaths and lie down, put the palms of your hands flat on the ground or floor, and allow all this energy to drain into the earth. If you feel lightheaded, lie still a while longer, and when you get up, eat something made of grain (crackers, tortillas, pretzels, popcorn, bread, for example) and drink some water.

This little ritual is especially effective when done by a group of women on the night of the full moon. You'll know you embody the Goddess.

Part 2

A Very Brief History of Modern Feminist Spirituality

Witches and Pagans and Druids

When the Parliament of the World's Religions gathered in 1893, representatives of Western Christianity, both Roman Catholic and Protestant, were present, as were a Jewish delegation and a few Friends, Shakers, Eastern Orthodox Christians, Buddhists, and Hindus. Mormons were not invited, Native Americans were represented by an anthropologist, and only one African Methodist Episcopal bishop and one Unitarian laywoman gave presentations. As the author of the history of the Parliament comments, "aside from a strong dose of Anglo-Saxon triumphalism, issues linked to the question of ethnicity were... muted."[1]

When the Parliament met again in 1993, the world had changed. In addition to the religions listed above, Baha'i, Islam, Jainism, Shinto, Sikhism, Taoism, Zoroastrianism, and African traditional religions were represented.

And the Witches were there! In the *SourceBook* we can read a two-page "Portrait of Wicca" and, in a sidebar, the "Charge of the Goddess."

---

1. Richard Hughes Seager, "A Legacy Worth Celebrating," in *A SourceBook for the Community of Religions*, edited by Joel Beversluis (Chicago: The Council for a Parliament of the World's Religions, 1993), pp. 4–9. Note: The book has been rereleased by New World Library, May 2000.

It is said that when the Witches gave their presentation (a ritual), only a few of the most orthodox believers felt compelled to leave the room.

While television sitcoms and shocker movies more often than not portray Witches in silly, erroneous, or unfavorable ways, we have been gaining recognition as a legitimate religion during the past twenty years and have, in fact, been recognized as a legitimate religion since 1985.

In 1979, PBS reporter Margot Adler came out of the broomcloset, interviewed dozens of pagans, and wrote *Drawing Down the Moon*. The book's "real message," Adler wrote in her revised edition (1986), "is that the spiritual world is like the natural world — only diversity will save it." *Drawing Down the Moon,* she continues, "espouses radical polytheism.... It stands against all of the totalistic religious and political views that dominate our society. It says 'Strive to be comfortable on chaos and complexity.'... Polytheism always includes monotheism," she concludes. "The reverse is not true."[2]

In 1993, Cynthia Eller built upon Adler's work with her superb sociological study, *Living in the Lap of the Goddess*. Based on ten years of observation of "the movement" as it manifests in rituals, classes, workshops, retreats, and literature, Eller concludes that spiritual feminists exhibit at least three of five major characteristics: (1) we value women's empowerment, (2) we practice ritual and/or magic, (3) we revere nature, (4) we use "the feminine or gender as a primary mode of religious analysis," and (5) we espouse "the revisionist version[3] of Western history favored by the movement."

Eller also learned that most of the women who live in the lap of the Goddess are white and Anglo-Saxon, that most of us are refugees from Christian or Jewish childhoods, and that many of us are lesbians (though

---

2. Margot Adler, *Drawing Down the Moon: Witches, Druids, Goddess-Worshippers, and Other Pagans in America Today,* revised and exanded edition (Boston: Beacon Press, 1986), pp. vii–viii.
3. See appendix A.

not necessarily separatists). Most of us see ourselves as alienated from normal American society. We "came home" to the Goddess after attending a public event or reading one of the ovular[4] books, like Starhawk's *The Spiral Dance* or Miriam Zimmer Bradley's *The Mists of Avalon*.[5]

"I Am a Witch"

If we took a survey, we could probably find as many definitions of the word *Witch* as there are people who use it. Twenty years ago, for example, we were told to say *I am a Witch* three times and really think about what we were saying. We imagined that made us witches.

When the Latin word *pagan* came into English in the late Middle Ages, it meant "civilian," as opposed to *miles*, "soldier." In their early literature, Christians called themselves *milites*, "enrolled soldiers of Christ." Our currently favored definition, that pagans are *non-Christian countryfolk* didn't come into use until the mid-sixteenth century. While the medieval Fathers of the Church had seized Greek and Roman literature to attack what they saw as idolatry and infidelity, by the time of the Renaissance the classical pagans were much admired and their mythology was revived in humanism, art, and literature.[6]

As *pagan* is commonly used by present-day self-described pagans, the word generally refers to anyone who is not a member of one of

---

4. *Ovular*, like *thealogy, hera,* and *herstory*, is a word used by feminist writers (some of whom are men) as an alternative to the outdated masculinist nouns.

5. Cynthia Eller, *Living in the Lap of the Goddess: The Feminist Spirituality Movement in America* (New York: Crossroad, 1993). The list of five major characteristics appears on page 6; the other information I cite is in chapter 2 of her book. Please note that while I use the first person pronoun here, Eller sticks to third person. *The Spiral Dance* is now available in a twentieth anniversary edition, and there are now two prequels to *The Mists of Avalon*.

6. *Oxford Universal Dictionary*, p. 1414. See also Jean Seznec, *The Survival of the Pagan Gods: The Mythological Tradition and Its Place in Renaissance Humanism and Art*, translated by Barbara F. Sessions (Princeton, N.J.: Princeton University Press, 1995).

the standard-brand religions, although Buddhists, Hindus, and Native Americans do not like to be called pagans. A *neo-pagan* is someone whose religion is earth-based and focuses on a Mother down here with us instead of a Father way up there far away from us. Followers of the nouveau-Norse traditions, especially Asatru, like to call themselves *heathens*.

The word *Wicca* is said to come from Middle English words that mean "wise" and/or "to bend." (If you have access to the *American Heritage Dictionary*, you can follow the etymology back to the word's Indo-European roots. You will learn marvelous things.) A Wiccan is therefore someone who wisely bends power. People who use the word Wicca to describe themselves are generally more High-Church (see below) than I am.

A *Witch* is someone who accepts the reality of the Great Goddess who was worshipped 30,000 or more years ago. A Witch worships Her today. Many Witches also worship Her son/consort, the many-named God. I have also met people who avoid The Dreaded W-Word altogether and call themselves Gaians, Druids, or use other nonloaded names.

A caution and a reminder: This is only my version of the nomenclature. You're likely to get other definitions from every Witch, Wiccan, or neo-pagan you talk to.

So why use the word *Witch?* It seems to be a scary word, with all its connotations of green skin and spells and evil decrepitude. *Wiccan* is less threatening, but like some other Witchy authors, I prefer the blunter word. "Witch" gets people's attention. As I am a kind, intelligent person, I can demonstrate to the world that "wicked" does not automatically define "Witch." By saying I'm a Witch, I can help restore honor to the women accused, persecuted, and murdered during the Burning Times. When I tell you I'm a Witch, I'm telling you my religion.

High-Church and Low-Church Witchery and the Goddess Stream

It is also important here to differentiate between what I call High-Church Witchery and Low-Church Witchery. I'll use an analogy to Western Christianity to explain these concepts.

Consider Roman Catholic or High-Church Anglican organization and practice. High-Church organization is episcopal, or top-down from the bishop. This is the familiar pyramid we also see in business, with the Big Man on top, row upon row of mid-level managers, and all the workers at the bottom. In a High Church, High Mass is celebrated in very formal language (Latin or formal English) before a traditional altar upon which sit the traditional implements (cross, candles, platen and chalice) in their traditional places. The order of service has been followed with little alteration for hundreds of years, and priestly vestments are likewise unchanged since the Middle Ages. Such a ritual, with its candles and incense and music, is beautiful to behold and truly inspiring to its believers.

Compare Gardnerian Wicca, established in 1939 (the same year *The Wizard of Oz* was released) with the initiation of Gerald B. Gardner and constructed over the next twenty years by Gardner with the help of Doreen Valiente and a number of prominent English ceremonial magicians, including Co-Masons and Rosicrucians.[7] With its priestly lineages, hierarchies of initiatory degrees, and secret names and titles, Gardnerian Wicca is highly organized, and Gardnerians also use a traditional altar and follow a scripted, formal ritual order. Recitations from the traditional Book of Shadows are highly serious. Led by its high priest (HP) and high priestess (HPs), a full-on Gardnerian ritual is very much the beautiful, impressive High-Church service.

Back to Christianity: the lower churches tend to be congregational, that is, run by committee or by the whole, the clergy often being

---

7. See Aidan A. Kelly, *Crafting the Art of Magic: Book I, A History of Modern Witchcraft, 1939–1964* (St. Paul, Minn.: Llewellyn, 1991), p. xvi. Although Kelly has been criticized, this book is worth reading.

elected or hired. Low-Church services consist of long and enthusiastic sermonizing in plain English, and lots of congregational participation, including call and response readings and singing the old, familiar hymns.

Low-Church Witchery is likewise congregational, covens and circles being largely autonomous, and ritual planning and creation are passed around the circle. Members participate in the ritual by purifying the space, calling in the quarters, doing divinations, leading meditations, and drumming or dancing. Guests are welcomed (and frequently put to work) and everybody gets to help decorate the altar.

Low-Church Witchery also tends to blend into what I'm coming to term the "Goddess stream." The Goddess stream is almost entirely female, showing very little interest in male energy (human or divine) and its thealogy (see note on page 33) is largely based on the work of a number of wise-women, the best known of whom are Z. Budapest, mother of Dianic Wicca, Vicki Noble, cocreator of the Motherpeace tarot, Marija Gimbutas, recoverer of the living goddesses of Old Europe, and Starhawk, author and activist. Every woman who finds the Goddess and writes about Her, whether the book is scholarly or poetic, adds to the stream. When I asked her about Dianic Wicca, Z. Budapest told me that it is "totally free of any dogma" and based on improvisation, which allows for variations. It seems to me, also, that women in the Goddess stream have less use for the usual magical tools than other Witches. Vicki Noble, for example, told me that she does not use them, nor does she cast a circle of four directions. Many women, of course, do use the Gardnerian implements and directions. They usually refer to themselves as eclectic, and their rituals tend to be unencumbered by tradition. Though she does not use the term, it is the Goddess stream that Eller describes in *Living in the Lap of the Goddess*.[8]

---

8. Z. Budapest in personal communication, December 21, 1999. Vicki Noble in personal communication, December 23, 1999.

A Very Brief History of Modern Feminist Spirituality

Saying that in the United States there is more Low-Church Witchery, which includes the solitary Witches, than High-Church, is probably a safe generalization, for we look with great suspicion upon hierarchy. We have taken to heart what our writers say about adding spontaneity to our rituals. Though we follow a ritual order, we frequently change things at will and make a lot of it up as we go along. Spontaneity can be a mixed blessing, however; while it can revitalize a tired formality, it can also lead to confusion when people don't really know what they're doing. That's why leadership and training in the basics are useful no matter which Witchery you prefer.

Covens and Circles

The coven is the basic unit of neo-pagan organization, and the ideal size is said to be thirteen people, though I don't think I've ever seen a group precisely that size. Starhawk says that a coven is like an affinity group, that is, people who know each other well and meet to share ideas and interests.[9] What a coven is not, however, is a surrogate family, a recovery group, a setting for group psychotherapy, or a political action group, although it can temporarily become any of these. What a coven is, is a group of people who meet to worship and work magic together.

Where does the word *coven* come from? When I looked it up in Doreen Valiente's *An ABC of Witchcraft*, I learned that some people believe the word came into English in 1662 in the "confession" of a Scottish Witch named Isobel Gowdie. Others cite the earlier trial of Dame Alice Kyteler of Kilkenny, where twelve people are named, the thirteenth being one Robin Artisson, their "devil." Still others refer to Margaret Murray's books, one of which contains an illustration of a dozen witches dancing with Robin Goodfellow. Valiente says that

---

9. Starhawk in workshop in Santa Monica, California, on December 11–12, 1999.

Chaucer uses the word *covent* in his *Canterbury Tales* (1387) to mean a group of thirteen people, adding that *covent* is a variant spelling of *convent* and survives to this day as the name of the London opera house, Covent Garden. An earlier fourteenth-century poem tells of a *coveyne* of thirteen people who danced in the churchyard while the priest was saying Mass. "Eventually," Valiente concludes, "the word 'coven' came to be used exclusively of the witches' cult group; and so it has come down to our day."[10]

In our day we also have what are called "cyber covens." These are composed of people who gather via the Net and the Web and declare themselves to be a coven. They email and post to each other and hold cyber rituals.

I'm not convinced this can work. A major element of ritual — indeed, of Witchery in general — is the manipulation of energy. When you're face to face with another Witch, or holding hands in a circle, you come to know the energy of that person. You work together to hold the energy of the circle. Energetics, as this manipulation of energy is called, is a vital part of spell-casting and other magical work, and as far as I can tell, the only energetics in a cyber-coven is electronic. I welcome email and I can't imagine not knowing my friends around the country (many of whom I've never met in person), but I don't do magic with them. Even though I sometimes believe that there is neither time nor space in the true reality behind the reality of our everyday lives, I don't see how it's possible to do cyber magic. You gotta have a coven where you spend time together, with your physical, mental, emotional, and spiritual presences *all in the same room.*

It is also worth noting that whereas the word *coven* seems to be preferred by High-Church Witches, Low-Church folks seem to prefer

---

10. Doreen Valiente, *An ABC of Witchcraft Past and Present* (Custer, Wash.: Phoenix Publishing, 1973), pp. 69–72.

the word *circle*. I can't explain the reason for this, except to note that *circle* sounds less hierarchical.

Green Spring Circle, a Fictitious Coven

To see what kinds of people become Witches, let us make up a coven. We'll call it Green Spring Circle. The circle, which has been in existence for about five years, was founded by five women who had taken a class together. Within a year, one of them dropped out because she thought her circle sisters weren't paying enough attention to her needs. By its next anniversary, the circle had grown to ten, a year later it was up to fourteen, last year it was down to nine, and now there are seven members. Such growth and attrition are not unusual. Women (and men, though there are fewer men in these Low-Church circles than in High-Church Witchery or ceremonial magic) come together to get their psychological needs met as much as anything else, and when something doesn't work, instead of working it out, they tend to leave. This is not cynicism speaking; it's what really happens.[11] Look at it this way: a circle of Witches is like a kaleidoscope. Give it a tap, shake it up, and a new pattern forms, as beautiful as before but different.

Green Spring Circle is led by Celeste and Madeleine (Maddy), a lesbian couple. Celeste, the mother of a grown son and daughter, is an executive assistant in a large corporation, where she is both closeted and broomclosed. Maddy is the office manager at a machine shop, where she is way out. Both women are healers (Celeste is an herbalist, Maddy a Reiki master), craftswomen (excuse me — craft*swimmin*), and drummers. Celeste is forever taking classes and thus has some training in Gardnerian Wicca, Dianic Wicca, Strega, the Demetrian Mysteries, and most of the psychic sciences.

---

11. If you want to make your circle or coven work, an excellent guidebook is Amber K's *Covencraft: Witchcraft for Three or More* (St. Paul, Minn.: Llewellyn, 1998). Another book I like is Jean Shinoda Bolen's *The Millionth Circle: How to Change Ourselves and The World* (Berkeley, Calif.: Conari Press, 1999).

Alicia Ravenwing (Raven) claims Mayan, Aztec, and Apache ancestry. She lives in a primitive cabin in one of the still-wild canyons of eastern Orange County, works in a garden center, and volunteers at a pet shelter. Every August she travels to Canyon de Chelly to commune with "the ancestors." Raven is also one of those pagans who run on "pagan time," which means if the ritual is scheduled to start at 7:30, that's what time she leaves home. Because her circle sisters love her, they put up with it.

Elbereth (her parents still call her Mary Ellen) is a single mother with a two-year-old daughter named Starling, whose first words — no kidding — were "blessed be." A college senior and theater major, Elbereth began meditating with a mixed group of American Buddhists in her early teens but became disillusioned when the guru kept buying Rolls-Royces while his people rode bicycles. She "just happened" to find books by Z. Budapest and Vicki Noble in the university library. A published poet, she also writes the public rituals Green Spring Circle stages with the other groups that are members of their Covenant of the Goddess local council. When Starling comes to rituals (which is most of the time), she is frisky, but she has learned to stop hurling herself upon the beauty of the altar. Starling's best friend is Maddy.

Hazel, ten years older than the others and divorced, is a middle manager at a computer company. When she recently had hip replacement surgery and learned that she also has osteoporosis, Celeste and Maddy began helping her with herbs and Reiki. Like the majority of neo-pagans, Hazel came to the Goddess from the New Age. She says she picked up *The Spiral Dance* "by mistake" in the Unity bookstore one Sunday, started reading, and couldn't put it down. She soon knew she'd "come home" and asked around to find like-minded women. She met Maddy in a computer store, but they don't remember how their conversation came around to the Goddess.

Christine is married to an aerospace engineer, Don, (a second marriage for both) and does not work outside her home. When they lived in St. Louis, they were Gardnerians, but since his transfer to Southern California, Don has become an intermittent Solitary. Their fifteen-year-old daughter, Donna, is more interested in boys than in the Goddess, so Christine came to Green Spring Circle for its community of women.

R'becca, an artist, does temporary office work to pay the rent and has temped in various divisions of Celeste's company. To her most often falls the responsibility of creating the most beautiful altar possible, and she brings flowers, crystals, goddess figures, candleholders, and scarves and drapes. She calls herself the circle's bag lady. Because she was an abused wife, she volunteers several nights a week on a domestic abuse hotline.

Death has recently touched Green Spring Circle; founding member Nancy died from metastasized breast cancer last year. They held a memorial ritual at which they planted a tree and named a star for her.

We'll check in on Green Spring Circle from time to time to see how they create altars and rituals and deal with the issues that touch us all.

Leadership and Hierarchy

A major issue, especially among us Low-Church rebels, is leadership. Nearly everywhere we look, in business, politics, and every other aspect of society, it's the old pyramid, with someone on top and the rest of us down below. We look at the academic world. Ditto. We look at the standard-brand religions. Ditto again. We look at High-Church Witchery. Still ditto. Is there such a thing as true participatory democracy? Can we get away from what Starhawk calls "power-over" and actually move into "power-with"?[12] Down with the hierarchs, we mutter to each other; up with consensus.

---

12. The best discussion of these thorny issues that I know is in Starhawk's *Truth or Dare: Encounters with Power, Authority, and Mystery* (New York: Harper & Row, 1987).

But it's not that easy. First, we're still too much a part of the society we're trying to heal. The pyramid world seethes with pecking orders and turf wars, and that's the baggage we drag, willy-nilly, into our circles. Second, let's face it, some people are natural leaders and others are natural followers. I've tried to work in groups where everyone tries to take charge and in other groups where no one wants to take any responsibility, though they're certainly willing to complain when anything goes wrong. Neither of these situations looks pretty. Third, discussion to get consensus can take a lot of tact and time, both of which are in short supply, especially when you're discussing something as trivial as should you put the veggies to the right or left of the meat dishes on the potluck table or what color candles should we use on the Imbolc altar. (I've heard both of these discussions. Usually, someone explodes: "Dammit, just use the white candles.")

Anarchy leads only to more anarchy, and without adequate leadership our religion simply cannot survive and grow. We need to let our natural leaders do what they know how to do. At the same time, however, if someone decides she wants to try on a leadership role — perhaps for the first time in her life — we must give her both support and a safe place.

Who are our leaders? People who know how to make mature decisions and deal with the consequences, both intended and unintended. People who already know how to write a ritual, set up an altar, manipulate energy, lead a spiral dance, construct costumes and props. People who understand the importance of delegation and are not afraid to share. People who aren't afraid to let others see their clay feet. People who can set aside control issues and get the job done with perfect love, perfect trust, and harm to none.

Is that too much to ask?

Coming Home to the Goddess

We Witches and other children of the Goddess have come to her by many and various paths. Like the women in Green Spring Circle, we became unhappy with the limitations of the standard-brand religions. So we explored meditation, which often led us to Buddhism in its many varieties or to the wonders of Hinduism, where the Mother is honored above (and at the root of) all others. Some of us tried the mainstream metaphysical churches, Christian Science, Science of Mind, Unity, but were not satisfied with a Father/Mother God who still looked like a man. Others of us turned to Native American spirituality, only to be disappointed in the most popular (and highly paid) "shamans." Some of us discovered sisterhood when we took classes called "Cakes for the Queen of Heaven" and "Rise Up and Call Her Name" at the local Unitarian-Universalist Church. And many of us simply worked our way through the local library or metaphysical bookstore until we came to a book that resonated in our hearts and minds.

By the time we found like-minded people, of course, we were usually grown up. Only now are very young children like Starling being raised in the Goddess religion.

Celeste, Maddy, and Nancy came to the Goddess after they attended a public ritual, saw a flyer, and took a class together. Raven used to worship at a Native American Christian church but found that the "chief" focused too much on himself; even so, she brings her "medicine" to the circle. Before Hazel came to the Goddess, she was a mainstream metaphysician, first in Christian Science, then in Unity. She wanted to find a God who looked more like her. Before she learned to meditate, Elbereth grew up without any faith at all. She wants to raise her daughter with a concept of higher and inner worlds. R'becca has spent time as an agnostic, an atheist, and a Unitarian (which her stepmother thinks are all the same thing). Christine grew up Lutheran, at her first marriage considered conversion to Judaism, and turned to Gardnerian Wicca when she met her first HPs at a lecture on quantum physics and magic.

Because Witches honor diversity and because we need to get along in the world even as we're trying to change it, I think it's important to honor every step we take as we walk along what one of my friends calls our lifepath. We need to know where we came from and understand why what we formerly believed no longer works. Without attacking or preaching to those who still find comfort in churches we've discarded, we need to examine why we have come home to the Goddess. We also need to understand that what we believe and practice today will evolve and change.

Reader, take some time now to do an inventory of your own path of faith. If you're anything like me, you've come to your present belief along a winding path. I was born into a Calvinist church and explored the nooks and crannies of New Thought, metaphysics, and Eastern religions before I came to the Goddess. I have been a Unitarian and a ceremonial magician, and I have studied the Aramaic origins of the Bible. In the decade since I started writing books about the Goddess, I've come further along Her path, and I do not doubt for a minute that my thealogy and cosmology will continue to evolve.

A Ritual for the Path of My Faith

If you have any physical souvenirs (like your christening gown or Sunday school attendance pins or Unitarian Universalist Association card), gather them and lay them in chronological order in a wide zigzag (snake track) in front of you. If all you've kept are the memories, write names or vignettes on paper or cards and lay them on the floor. If you have memories or fantasies from former lives, add them to the path.

Finally, get something that symbolizes your present life and faith and hold it in both hands. This could be a pine cone, a Goddess image, or a tool you use in your work. I might hold my computer mouse (which I have actually dedicated as a sacred tool, because to me it's as sacred as a wand or cauldron). What you hold could also be a handful of "empty" space that only appears to be empty, for it is really full of consciousness. Take a few minutes to find the perfect thing to represent your current life and faith.

Sit comfortably, facing your past and holding your present, and read the following words or tape them beforehand and listen to them or use them as a model to make up your own words.

> I face the path of my faith.
> This is the way I've come,
> the journey my soul has taken
> to bring me where I am today.
> I recall the people I've met on this path,
> teachers all,
> kind or unkind.
> They walked with me awhile,
> showed me their paths,
> and so I bless their teaching.
> I remember events and encounters along the way,
> pleasant or painful,
> always instructive —
> Whatever happened, it was useful,
> and in its own integrity was beautiful.
> But I have learned to follow my own path,
> I have learned where I must go.
> I bless the path of my past.

Still holding the symbol of your present, turn around. Turn your back on your past. Put it behind you.

> Holding my present in my own hands,
> I face my future.
> Every day I step forward on an unknown path,
> a unique path sprinkled with the star stuff
> of the Goddess.
> In Her presence, past, present, future are one time
> and here I am,
> where I'm supposed to be —
> now and always:
> my path is in Her.

Close your eyes and think about what this means to you. If you want to, begin writing a journal of your thinking about what you believe and how you express your belief.

Part 3

Practicing Her Presence Today

Worship

As we live our everyday lives, we find ourselves engaging more and more in worship. Before it becomes action, worship is focus; it is what is called *mindfulness*. To some people worship means keeping an "attitude of gratitude," and to others worship is seeing the "worth-ship" in life. It's creating altars and making music. It's saying, *I love and cherish all forms of life because I recognize something of which I am a part, and I want to celebrate my recognition.*

We can worship in a specifically demarcated holy place or we can worship just about anywhere on our planet, which is itself a holy place. We can sit or stand before our own altar and understand how an altar is a miniature earth that embodies all the earthly, earthy powers. We can worship with silent prayer, do a private ritual in our bedroom first thing in the morning, or gather and hold hands with like-minded and like-hearted people to strengthen our connections with one another and with all our kin on earth.

Since we don't know, however, exactly how people living as far back as the Stone Age worshipped the Goddess, we who live today have to use our best guesses about the ancient forms of worship. We use our intuition, our vision, and hints and suggestions from many sources, including archaeological discoveries and evidence from books in which the old ways were described in order to anathematize them.

This makes us a very eclectic bunch, and when we worship we often make it up as we go along. That's one reason why there are so many traditions and processes, so many ways of doing rituals (which all seem to work), and so many books that seem to contradict each other. I believe that they really complement each other. I believe that Witchery, or Wicca, is catholic in the original sense of the word: general and all-inclusive. Whatever our method of worship, what we're doing is practicing the presence of the Goddess.

As we dance with our Mother Earth to welcome the Age of Aquarius (or the New Age or the New Millennium), therefore, more and more people are wondering if the things we measure only with our minds and machines are enough to nourish our lives. We're asking if the things we buy and sell are what we really want, after all. We're looking for the invisible, nourishing dimension of life that hasn't been really accessible since the Industrial Revolution lined us all up and started whirring, cranking, and belching at us. We've been reaching forward to new and improved technology or backwards to the phony, sitcom-induced "traditional family values." But I wonder…have we been reaching in the right direction?

What would happen if we reached inward instead? If we laid hands on the small, dark, precious seeds of creativity and love that rest deep inside us all? Instead of focusing on outward things, what would happen if we focused inward?

Re-creating the Sacred Dimension

Whatever form our worship takes, our intention is to do what more and more people are doing: re-creating the sacred dimension in their lives, in life itself. We are renewing our personal connection to the divine.

As far as we can tell from the archaeological evidence, the Neolithic Civilization of the Goddess lived closer to the earth than we do today. They probably called her Mama back then and lived in harmony with the light and the dark, observing and celebrating the phases of the moon and the year. We who are creating the new earth-based religions — we who are their modern children — are inventing modern versions of ancient observations and celebrations.

We're observing and celebrating the re-emergence of open worship of the Goddess. To use the current jargon, we're seeing new patterns and changing our paradigms. We're merging the sacred with the secular. We're recalling our true essence, which is both immanent and transcendent. We're engaged in life both as it is and as it can be.

Have we come back again to paradox? Yes, indeed. It's difficult to write about the sacred dimension because words are intrinsically inadequate to the job. In writing this book, I'm using a left-brain medium to approach a right-brain process, and what comes out are paradox and extravagant language. But you'll also find paradox and extravagant language in books on Zen and yoga and the Qabalah, in Sufi and Hassidic mysticism, in the words of the Christian and New Thought mystics, and in the *Course in Miracles* books.

I think this fact helps to explain why most of the books on Goddess ritual are like cookbooks: it's easier to give a recipe than to wander around in the batter. How do we describe the indescribable? How do we visualize the unseeable, apprehend the impalpable, ponder the unthinkable?

As simply as I can say it, the practice of the presence of the Goddess is a way to get centered in your own center. Other people have other names for this center: God, Christ Consciousness, Higher Self, Nirvana, Unity With All, Reverence For Life. I call this center the Goddess.

Of the many paths that lead us to the Goddess, I believe that the following four are the most familiar and relevant.

Deep Thought

The first path is largely intellectual. We need intellectual content — facts, history, theory, philosophy, thealogy — and intelligent discussion of that content so we don't fall into silliness or rote repetition of practices handed down from some god or guru or would-be highest of all high priestesses. We need to think for ourselves. We need to think about what we're doing, not do it just because someone said we should. When you adopt a mystical sensibility, therefore, do not abandon your common sense. Keep your wits about you and throw some healthy skepticism in the mix.

 A Ritual of Thoughtfulness

Take a few minutes to find out what's on your mind. What are you currently reading? What are you thinking about these days? What has been bothering you? What do you need to learn? What questions do you hear yourself asking? If you need to, sit down with a tablet and pencil and make a list. From your list, select one topic[1] that seems to need resolution, or at least direction.

Set up your altar. If you have a figure of Athene, set Her in the center. You can also set anything else that signifies Deep Thought to you on your altar, but I never put books on an altar where there are lighted candles.

Holy Powers of Elemental Air, goddesses and gods of the mind,
I seek intellectual understanding,

---

1. For all four of these little rituals, if you have more topics on your list, do more rituals. Your rituals will be clearer if you focus on one topic per ritual.

I seek to know [name your issue].
Holy Powers of Intellectual Understanding,
Come into my life, touch my every step, bless me with your
Gifts of reason, judgment, discrimination, the fresh air of new ideas.
Great and generous Powers,
I need to know,
I need to think,
I need to understand.

Now put these thorny issues out of your conscious mind. Read a mystery, watch your favorite video, go to work. At the same time, know that the deities work in mysterious ways. Remain alert for hints and leads and suggestions. Perhaps you'll overhear a conversation that jogs your mind, perhaps someone will mention a book or magazine to you — however it happens, you will receive food for thought. Think about it.

Good Works

The second path is more active. No one I know is as dedicated and selfless as Mother Teresa or Albert Schweitzer, to be sure, but we can do good works wherever we live on the planet. We can do them out of kindness and the recognition that we're all related, and not out of that old-time fear that we won't go to heaven if we don't. We can be courteous to our coworkers, yield on the freeway, volunteer to feed the homeless on a national holiday, or give money to a charity. Even our smallest good works are beneficial. They're not only mutually beneficial, but they also add that much more kindness to the aura of the planet. Believe me, kindness is even more important today than it was five or ten years ago.

A Ritual of Good Work

Homelessness and social turmoil. Floods and tornadoes. World hunger and the uncountable number of children living in poverty. It seems as if there's no end of calls for us to do good works in the world. What issues touch your heart? What causes would inspire you to actually do something? Do you care about Tibet or seemingly insurmountable problems in African nations? Wait — let's stay closer to home. Do you have a friend with cancer or AIDS? Do you actually notice the homeless and hungry people in your town?

Again, take some time to sit down with a tablet and pencil and find out what you would like to better understand. Perhaps you can sort through the appeals you received in the mail this week. Select a cause you really care about and are ready to do something about.

Set up your altar. Perhaps you will want to lay a photo of a philanthropist or activist you admire on it, or perhaps a figure of Aphrodite, who is not just a goddess of love but the Divine Creatrix.

> Holy Powers of Elemental Earth, goddesses and gods of the
>   manifest world,
> I seek understanding of the purpose of charity, of good works,
> I seek to know [name your issue].
> Holy Powers of Practical Understanding,
> Come into my life, touch my every step, bless me with your
> Gifts of groundedness in the Goddess, of survival and prosperity.
> Great and generous Powers,
> I need to know,
> I need to take action,
> I need to understand.

Now go about your daily life. Put your yearning to do big good works aside and do the small works: weed and water your garden, clean out those overstuffed closets, sharpen and polish your tools and hang them in their proper places. Opportunities for philanthropy will come to you. Perhaps you'll get a mail appeal that inspires you. Perhaps you'll get a phone call from a politician who finally makes sense. Perhaps a friend will invite you to a lecture or other event that makes you stand up and stand for something. Go for it.

Experiential Play

The third path is both active and intellectual. This is the scientific path (maybe it's technological as well), and ritual may be its most obvious application. An experientially oriented person does enough research to create a ritual with the correct associations and actions, does the ritual according to a written plan, and makes notes on performance and outcome. On the experiential path tread ceremonial magicians and other people who manipulate realities to get results.

Some people make a big fuss, however, about "manipulative" magic, which they see as magic that makes people do what they don't want to do. Such magic is rightly a Big No-No, but the underlying issues are control and coercion, and these are ego-magic.

There's nothing wrong with manipulation. Any time you're *doing something,* you're being manipulative. That is, you're operating or controlling something by the skilled use of your hands. This is true when we hold a pencil and make letters, when we cook or scrub or sew, when we cast a circle. We need to understand that *all magic* is *manipulative,* whether you're doing it with your mind (visualization) or your hands. The word comes from the Latin, *manipulus,* "handful," which comes from *manus,* "hand."[2] Related words are "manual" (as in "manual

---

2. See the "Toe-To-Toe" piece on this topic I wrote with Anne Niven in *PanGaia* #21 (Autumn 1999), pp. 20–23

labor") and "manufacture." There's no gender issue here, either. "Man" in Latin is *vir*, whence comes *virtue*.

Because the magical scientists (also called *magi*) are such highly serious people most of the time, I call the path Experiential Play to remind us all to take it seriously without becoming too solemn. Mistakes and laughter are a valuable part of the process.

A Ritual to Manipulate Reality

Do your rituals work? Are you having any kind of experience with the other realities? How are you getting along in your everyday reality? Do you have power issues, control issues? Do you spend too much time trying to get people to do things? What is happening in your world?

Sit down with your tablet and pencil and write about what's going on in your life. What issues or lessons or challenges seem to be coming up again and again and again? As before, select just one topic or issue.

Build your altar. In the center, place a figure of Brigit or items that symbolize creativity to you — your computer mouse, a block of wood or stone waiting to reveal what can be carved from it, a box of crayons or fingerpaints.

> Holy Powers of Elemental Fire, goddesses and gods of creativity,
> I seek understanding of the nature of reality and the purpose of
>   change,
> I seek to know [name your issue].
> Holy Powers of Inventive Understanding,
> Come into my life, touch my every step, bless me with your
> Gifts of passion, enlightenment, growth, and transformation,
> Great and generous Powers,
> I need to know,

I need to see what is real,
I need to understand.

As you move though the world you live and work and play in, watch yourself. Watch other people. See if you can see energies, your own, theirs, the energies of groups, the energies of things most people consider inanimate. Do not take action. Simply observe. And as you move through the world, energies will arise where you least expect them, unexplained things will happen. You will become more aware. You will learn that you can change your own reality without controlling other people all the time. *Pay attention.*

Devotion

The fourth path, like deep thought, can be passive and, like anything else, devotion can be taken to messy extremes. I see it as pure love, as an unconditional love that sees clearly and focuses on the center. Devotion needs to stay grounded, though, and sometimes it needs to be tough. It always requires a good dose of common sense.

A Ritual of Devotion

What is love? How many of its varieties are present in your life? What do you love? How do you express your love? Are your friendships deep and stable? Are you yearning to be partnered? Are you loving and beloved by anyone besides your dog or cat?

Sit down again with your tablet and pencil and write about love and its place in your life. Select an issue centering on love that you seek to understand.

As you build your altar, do so with care. Are you merely doing a job here, or is your altar a work of your love? If you have a figure of Isis or Kuan Yin, put Her in the center. You can also put other things that symbolize love on your altar.

> Holy Powers of Elemental Water, goddesses and gods of love,
> I seek understanding of what love really is,
> I seek to know [name your issue].
> Holy Powers of Emotional Understanding,
> Come into my life, touch my every step, bless me with your
> Gifts of steadfastness, tenderness, empathy, and compassion.
> Great and generous Powers,
> I need to know,
> I need to feel what love truly is,
> I need to understand.

As you do what you do in your everyday life, stop worrying about finding love or a new lover. Focus on doing what you do with attention. Take off your masks and be yourself, and be open to the thoughts and feelings and actions of other people. Instead of trying to draw love to yourself, focus on giving love. As any poet or novelist will tell us, love can come in unexpected ways, and even if love does not come to you, the world is still filled with it. All you need to do is feel it.

When we practice the presence of the Goddess, we follow all four of these paths at once. Sometimes we emphasize one path or another, but the ideal is balance. We need to add feeling to our thought and think about what we're feeling. We need to be mindful when we practice the presence of the Goddess.

What you've been doing after these little rituals, as you avoid focusing on your issue, is releasing the energy from your aura so the

Goddess (or the universe) can work on it. Remember — we are not always in control. Sometimes, however, we need to stay focused. In a magical or meditative context, such focus is called "mindfulness." Traditionally, mindfulness has meant focusing on a mantra, a yantra (visual symbol), or a chant or affirmation. I once had a friend, for example, who spent several months setting the alarm on her wristwatch to go off every five minutes. Every time the alarm sounded, she said a brief, silent prayer for herself and for the earth.

Let us enlarge this process: let's turn it into *rememberfulness* and get rid of the alarm. How? Try this. Go about your regular day at the office or the plant or at home, and do all things you normally do. At the same time, reserve one small, side corner of your mind to remember. Anytime you come to a stopping place, pull the contents of this small, side corner forward and remember. Remember who you are — a divine child, part of the consciousness of the planet, a member of a community. Remember where you are — sheltered by the flowing blue cloak of our Mother, living on the skin of an organism named Earth, living as a child of the oldest goddess, who is Gaia. Remember to give thanks for who you are and where you are.

With a split-second wordless thought or with a full-blown ritual as you live your everyday life, practice the presence of the Goddess.

One of the best books about mindfulness could be a Zen text, but it's really one of the best of the Christian mystical books: *The Practice of the Presence of God.*[3] This book contains the thoughts of Brother Lawrence, a humble monk who to this day is much beloved and admired because while he was scrubbing the floors of his abbey, doing laundry, cleaning the kitchen, repairing shoes, he gave his work to his God. He didn't argue or preach (though he did write spiritual letters),

---

3. Brother Lawrence of the Resurrection, *The Practice of the Presence of God,* edited and translated by John J. Delaney (New York: Doubleday Image Book, 1977).

and he didn't do anything spectacular. He just walked around in his life practicing the presence of his god, and that practice still spreads joy to all who encounter him, if only through his little book.

Try it yourself. Don't talk about what you believe to people who really aren't interested. Don't show off what you can do because you believe in something. Just walk around in your life remembering who you are and who She is.

In our own ways, we can all follow the example of Brother Lawrence. Let's keep the Goddess in mind. Let's take Her to work with us and remember to work as effectively and creatively as we can. Let's take Her shopping with us and buy healthful food and items with biodegradable or recyclable packaging, and — as long as people are hungry or homeless — let's try not to buy so many luxury goodies. Let's remember that She's everybody's mother when we're stuck in traffic or those Witnesses are knocking on the door early Sunday morning. Let's even keep Her at home with us.

Practicing Her Presence Every Day

Here is a to-do list of ways we can practice the presence of the Goddess in our daily lives.

Listen to music. Today there's more Goddess music than there was a decade ago. CDs and tapes are available in both metaphysical stores and mainstream stores (usually in the New Age music section), in several Websites (including amazon.com), in catalogs, and at New Age, Renaissance, Whole Earth, and Womanspirit fairs. Musicians also advertise in our magazines and sell CDs and tapes when they perform live.

Cure your addiction to the news ("all crime, all the time") and inane talk-radio by listening to Goddess music in your car. Start and end your day with it. I'm convinced it's better for your mental state than listening to the news. Note that I am certainly not suggesting that you give up knowing what's going on in the world. Such total naïveté can be hazardous to your health. What I'm suggesting is balance.

Find a healing scent you like and use it. Many herbs are associated with the Goddess, and many of them smell good. My favorite is vanilla, a feminine herb whose powers include love, lust, and mental powers. Carrying a vanilla bean is said to restore lost energy and improve the mind.[4] I burn vanilla candles, use vanilla essential oil and potpourri, and wear "Vanilla Fields" cologne. All this vanilla reminds me of the sweetness of the Goddess and makes me feel good. (It makes men think someone's been baking.)

Appreciate your friends, former friends, relations, and the animals who live with you. We're each of us created in Her image. The Goddess myths, older by thousands of years than the Genesis myth, describe how She gave birth to the universe and everything in it. (Well, as one who lives with two cats, I do not hold Her responsible for fleas.) In 1987, geneticists presented evidence that everyone living on earth today may be descended from an African "mitochondrial Eve." If her DNA lives in us all, it means we are truly related.[5]

Consider the love and support you exchange with your friends, the help and information you exchange both with coworkers and people you hardly know, the unconditional love and entertainment you receive from the animals that live with you. My cats give me stereo purring and kitty Reiki.

---

4. Scott Cunningham, *Cunningham's Encyclopedia of Magical Herbs* (St. Paul, Minn.: Llewellyn, 1988), p. 215, and other books on herbs.

5. John Tierney et al., "The Search for Adam and Eve," *Newsweek* (Jan. 11, 1988), pp. 46–52. To get more up-to-date information (including comments by Creationists), go to the Web, type "mitochondrial Eve," follow the links, and read your eyes out. It's fascinating.

Consider the lessons you've learned from the people who are no longer in your life, and why they're no longer in your life. Even people with whom you have had terrible quarrels taught you something, if only to get away and stay away from poisonous people.

But please don't fall into the metaphysical trap of thinking that everything that happens to you happens because you drew it to you so you could pay a karmic debt or learn a karmic lesson (whatever that means). Behind this kind of poisonous thinking lurks a more pernicious line of thought, which goes something like this: *if I drew all this to me, that means I must be really powerful and am somehow in control of the universe, but I must not be good enough to draw good stuff to me, so I punish myself by drawing bad stuff into my consciousness and life.*

Phooey. Remember that you are not the center of the universe. Use common sense when you recognize your lessons. Practice that good old "attitude of gratitude."

Redecorate your space. Put a fresh flower, a potted plant, a pretty shell, or a feather on your desk at work. Hang symbols of elemental fire, water, air, and earth on the walls at home. Set a candle in a beautiful holder and a goblet on a doily with a photo of your grandmother or a tarot card. Install a Goddess image — anyone from Isis or Athena to Miss Piggy or Barbie — in a place of honor in your home. Set up an altar and redecorate it for each major festival. Decorate your home as much as you can get away with.

Read good books and magazines.[6] As a visit to your local bookstore will show, there's a whole library of Goddess books already on the shelves and more on the way every day. Our magazines seem to come and go, but *SageWoman* and *Green Egg* are showing longevity. I also like

---

6. See appendix B, the Goddess 101 Basic Library, for books that I think are key to understanding who we are and what we're doing.

PanGaia, Circle Magazine, The Beltane Papers, New Moon Rising, Enchanté, The Crone Chronicles, and *New Moon* (a magazine for girls).

But don't just sit there and read passively. React to what you're reading. Talk back to the author, either in your mind, by writing notes in the margin (if you own the book), or by writing letters or email to the author. Synthesize what you learn in one book with what you learn in other books so you have a rounded vision and relatively bias-free information. If you choose to write to an author, you can send a letter to the publisher of the book, which will be forwarded, or you can communicate more directly via email. I did a small informal survey of some of the authors I know, asking them how they feel about receiving email from readers. Most of the authors I know love to receive email and reply to it. As Z. Budapest said, "Readers are cool." We learn a lot from you.

Log on to the Internet and the World Wide Web and explore. For example, here's how I just spent ten minutes. I went to www.pagan.com, www.witchvox.com, www.reclaiming.org, and www.cog.org and followed some of the links. At just one search engine, I found 419 sites listed when I typed "witch" and 259 when I typed "goddess." By the time this is published, those numbers may have doubled. The major publishers have Websites, as do catalogs (I especially love www.SacredSource.com), creative people, and teachers.

Experience the labyrinth. For thousands of years the labyrinths have been a primary symbol of the Sacred Center we call the Goddess. If you live near a labyrinth, walk it as often as you can. It's a powerful walking meditation. But you can also construct a "finger labyrinth"[7] that you can "walk" any time and in any weather, either ambient or emotional.

---

7. Instructions for constructing both Cretan and Chartres labyrinths are given in Melissa Gayle West, *Exploring the Labyrinth: A Guide to Healing and Spiritual Growth* (New York: Broadway Books, 2000). See also Lauren Artess, *Walking a Sacred Path: Rediscovering the Labyrinth As a Sacred Tool* (New York: Riverhead, 1995).

Take classes in women's spirituality. You might want to learn mask and rattle construction, drumming or belly dancing, beginning Wicca, herbalism and aromatherapy, jewelry making, weaving, creative writing, and divination (tarot, I Ching, or runes) or other psychic sciences. Before you sign up, however, ascertain the orientation of the teacher. You might not enjoy spending time with a macho astrologer or a musician who insists that drumming was invented by and for men.

Wear Goddess jewelry. If wearing a yoni or a labrys or a pentacle might be troublesome, try a simple crescent moon, a silver flower, or a ring with a meaningful but inconspicuous design. Keep in mind that you're not wearing this jewelry to advertise but to help you remember, and you may even prefer to wear your significant jewelry under your clothes. I wear a cowrie shell bracelet most of the time. In my ears I have an owl charm, the rune *fehu,* and a tiny Herkimer diamond, and I often wear my Blessed Bee[8] earrings. And I have finally bought a pentacle. It hangs from an owl charm, and few people even notice it. (So much for being in or out of the broomcloset!)

Put a bumpersticker on your car or wherever you want to make a statement. What the bumpersticker says, of course, may be dictated by where you live. LOVE YOUR MOTHER is fairly inoffensive, whereas WIZARDS HAVE CRYSTAL BALLS AND HALLOW WEINIES might get you more attention than you really want. The bumpersticker on my car says BRIGHT BLESSINGS, and the one on my CPU says SUBVERT THE DOMINANT PARADIGM.

Take action. Recycle (of course) and reduce your conspicuous consumption. Smile at other drivers on the freeway and say thank you to servers and busboys and clerks.

If you feel strongly about an issue, actually *do something about it.*

---

8. The Blessed Bees are Found power animals. There is more about Blessed Bees, including how to invoke them, at the end of this book (see page 123).

Write letters to the President and your Congressional delegation and your state and city representatives. Our Senators and Representatives have Websites; use them.

Send money to an organization whose work you feel is important, like gun control advocacy groups, so our kids won't be able to take guns to school, and environmental protection groups, so maybe our grandchildren will still have an environment. Join a local organization or a national one. Do volunteer work or take part in a demonstration for your cause. Boycott businesses that use child labor or clearcut forests. You can find enormous amounts of information on issues Witches should care about on the Web.

Look at art. Find art that honors women and art by women. Art is everywhere — paintings, prints, posters, sculpture, fiber art, found art, calendars. As you look at a piece of art, consider the courage of the woman who made it, think about what the art means (especially if it's feminist art, which can be beautiful and scary at the same time), and examine your own resonance with this art.

Create your own art. The act of creation is itself ritualistic because it alters your consciousness and is repetitive. The very essence of the Goddess is creation, and nothing She created is junk. Since we're all created in Her image or, as some believe, we're literally part of Her body because we're living creatures, everything we create is beautiful and precious, if only to our Mother. (Does She use divine refrigerator magnets to display our efforts?)

Multi-media art, or found art, can be more expressive than drawing or painting because it helps you see things in new ways. Found art means combining things you find — rocks, feathers, twigs, dried flowers and herbs, shells, the wishbone from your baked chicken. You can add ribbons, glitter, T-shirt paint (the kind that comes in squeeze bottles), beads of all kinds, fortune cookie fortunes, and orphan earrings. You don't need formal training or expensive tools. You can use white glue and string to hold things together, and your symbols can be traditional ones or personal ones that you thought up yourself.

A Ritual of Creativity

When you begin a new project — perhaps you have something specific in mind, like the creation of a new magical tool or a small symbol to suspend from your rearview mirror — and lay your materials out on your table or desk, your working space becomes an ad hoc altar. Unless anything is terribly flammable, light a candle and imagine a glowing circle around the room where you're working. Think about the work you're beginning, how it will grow and develop, who (besides you) it might touch. State your intention for this project out loud. Then read these words or tape them beforehand and listen to them or use them as a model to make up your own words.

> As She created from Herself
> a work of art
> and called it the universe,
> So do I create from the things I find
> my own work of art
> and call it remembrance.
> As She provided all these treasures
> for our nourishment and pleasure,
> So do I accept the things I find
> and use them to create new worlds.
> As She labored and played,
> So do I play and remember Her.

When you open your eyes, let your creative mind travel into your hands and begin to idly manipulate your found objects until something clicks.

You can do something as simple as tying multi-colored ribbons around the stem of a goblet or go for a project as complex as a wall-size collage of postcards, feathers, seed pods, and pieces of jewelry. Let yourself play. Several years ago, I combined a Champion spark plug, two white marbles, and some dried rosebuds on a maroon scallop shell. (Can you picture the configuration?) Heisenberg, the Green Man, and this fine upstanding fellow are the only gods I allow in my house.

It's said that fairies love ribbons. If you want to attract the Good Neighbors, or just hang something pretty in your room, get a smallish embroidery hoop and enough yard-long pieces of ribbon to go around the hoop, then glue one end of each piece of ribbon to the hoop. (It comes out looking like a windsock.) Use thread or more ribbon to make a hanger for the hoop. You can also add beads, bells, and feathers, and then hang it by a window to catch a breeze.

As you're working, be remberful. What is the significance of this feather or this acorn? Why are you using these colors of beads or ribbons or yarn? Are you working (playing) with curved or straight lines? Why? How does this process feel to you? How does this tiny ritual alter your consciousness? What are you going to do with your altered consciousness? You might want to write your answers to these questions in your journal.

Talk to yourself. Sing to yourself. We all do it all the time anyway. We're forever programming our minds to be either user-hostile or user-friendly. We're creating our own consciousness, and what we create in our own consciousness we also create in the consciousness of the planet. Wouldn't it be better for all of us if we used that self-talk to re-create the presence of the Goddess?

Self-talk has other names: mindfulness, silent prayer, awareness, meditation, affirmatory repetition. But it doesn't matter what you call it, so long as you just do it. When you're having one of *those days,* it's heartening to repeat a prayer by Dame Julian of Norwich, a medieval

English mystic: ALL WILL BE WELL, AND ALL WILL BE WELL, AND ALL MANNER OF THINGS WILL BE WELL. A few years ago I wrote a short story in which I paraphrased Dame Julian's prayer: ALL IS WELL, ALL SHALL BE WELL, ALL CAN ONLY BE WELL. Try repeating this after a hard day. Recall Sancta Chrona and know that as you are repeating these words, all is in fact well and tomorrow is another day.

You can choose one of the familiar mantras: OM. MA. MAMA. When you chant, the sound sets up vibrations and resonances that heal and transform your mind and body. If you chant subvocally, you don't get the quite the same transformatory effect, but, still, it clears your mind, which is useful in those times when you're feeling picked on or ignored or are otherwise wallowing in negative emotions. Because I love the Tibetan goddess Tara, I repeat Her mantra all through the day: OM TARE TUTARE SOHA.

You can also select a Goddess name and do a few minutes of research to find out what Her attributes and associations are. Then, keeping what you've learned in mind, sound Her name: ATHENA. ISIS. SAULE. BRIGIT. AMATERASU. Sound slowly, drawing out all vowel sounds, extending the consonant sounds as much as possible as well. AAAAAAAAAA-THEEEEEEEEE-NAAAAAA. Sound the name as long as your breath lasts (as you do this sounding, your breath capacity will grow) and let the sounds swirl around your throat, ears, and heart. Do it aloud in your car in traffic. Sound your Goddess name every morning in the shower, as loud as you want to, and sound it under your breath whenever you're doing anything that doesn't require complete, left-brain attention. (That is, sound the name of Juno Habundia before and after you balance your checkbook, but not during.)

When you're ready, move from self-talk and sounding Goddess names to chanting and singing. There must be hundreds of chants on CD and tape, and most of them are easy to learn. Teach the songs and chants you like to your friends and sing them in unison, in parts, or as rounds.

The chant to begin with is Deena Metzger's wonderful Goddess Chant: ISIS, ASTARTE, DIANA, HECATE, DEMETER, KALI, INANNA. I have heard two, very different, versions of this chant. One is in Charlie Murphy's CD *Catch the Fire,* and the other is in the CD *From the Goddess,* performed by Robert Gass and On Wings of Song.

Here are a few more Goddess chants:

By Buffy Ste. Marie: THE GODDESS IS ALIVE AND MAGIC IS AFOOT.

By Starhawk: SHE CHANGES EVERYTHING SHE TOUCHES, AND EVERYTHING SHE TOUCHES, CHANGES.

Attributed to Z Budapest and based on a chant, "We all come from the God," by Richard Quinn: WE ALL COME FROM THE GODDESS AND TO HER WE SHALL RETURN, LIKE A DROP OF RAIN FLOWING TO THE OCEAN.

From the Bloodrose Faerie Tradition: HOLY MOTHER, IN YOU WE LIVE AND MOVE AND HAVE OUR BEING.

From a group of women Starhawk once worked with: CAULDRON OF CHANGES, BLOSSOM OF BONE, ARC OF ETERNITY, HOLE IN THE STONE.

From the Requiem Mass of the Catholic Church, which many composers have set to music, BENEDICTA QUAE VENIT IN NOMINE DOMINAE. I have made it feminine. The Latin translates as "Blessed is She who comes in the name of the Lady." You can sing this to Andrew Lloyd Webber's powerful music.

There are also numerous Goddess songs. One of my favorites — actually a parody — was printed in the famous Great Goddess issue of *Heresies.*[9] It's sung to the familiar tune, "Jesus Loves Me."

---

9. Toni Head, "Changing Hymns to Hers," in *The Great Goddess, Heresies,* Vol. 2, No. 1, Issue 5, rev. ed., 1982, pp. 16–17.

Isis loves me, this I know
Mother God has told me so.
She is strong and so are we
Fighting for equality.
Yes, Isis loves me
Yes, Isis loves me
Yes, Isis loves me
Our Lady told me so.

Craftella

Speaking of parody, never hesitate to Find your own goddesses. Toward the end of one of our meetings last summer, someone in my local Covenant of the Goddess (CoG) chapter said, "Why don't you write something for the next newsletter?"

So I did.

Craftella is the celestial model of what a modern high priestess should be. She inspires and delights our inner children with beads and bubbles and nutritious potluck dishes and imparts useful principles of organization to all who listen to Her. A priestess who is truly guided by Craftella knows which chapter officer promised to do what and where the paperwork is. She can hold a meeting together and keep track of who "volunteered" to do which ritual.

Whenever the time is ripe, Craftella calls upon our souls to rise and come unto Her, for She is the soul of nature that gives life to the universe and writes the lyrics. Let us therefore sing a Song of Craftella. I'm sure you'll recognize the tune to Her song.

On the first night of Cogmonth,
Craftella gave to me
A hive for my Blessed Bee.
On the second night of Cogmonth,

Craftella gave to me
Two beaded scarves
And a hive for my Blessed Bee.
On the third night ... three green herbs
On the fourth night ... four direction sigils
On the fifth night ... five pentacles
On the sixth night ... six wands a-waving
On the seventh night ... seven knives a-pointing
On the eighth night ... eight drummers drumming
On the ninth night ... nine Green Men leafing
On the tenth night ... ten Maidens dancing
On the eleventh night ... eleven Mothers cooking
On the twelfth night ... twelve Crones complaining
On the full moon night of Cogmonth,
Craftella gave to me
A coven that will not talk back.

Traditions

Back in the olden days of Witchery (the early 1970s), when our new/old religion was still about half science fiction and half fantasy, we used to hear a lot about "traditions" that claimed roots on Arcturus or in Atlantis or at least in the New Forest. Back then, we yearned to be the children of traditional Witch families who had bravely preserved the Ancient Wisdom in pictures (as tarot cards) or coded books or via the sacred Oral Tradition. Back then, we needed to make such claims because they gave us increased respectability among the other neo-pagans. We thought we had to be at least as archaic as the Theosophists and the Spiritualists and the other mystical, magical sects that came into existence with the European Occult Revival of the late nineteenth century but which also claimed medieval, Egyptian, Chaldean, or outer-space antecedents.

I don't always believe what I read, however. I've learned that you can't always take people's claims at face value, no matter how much you like the person or the claim. So I did some research and learned that most of the traditions are in fact younger than I am (I was born in 1941).

> Here's a list, which is by no means exhaustive, of Wiccan and pagan traditions and authors whose books you can read: Ar nDraiocht Fein (neo-Druid, Isaac Bonewits), Aglaian, Alexandrian (Stewart and Janet Ferrar), Algard, Asatru (Edred Thorssen), Bluestar, Church of Wicca (Gavin and Yvonne Frost), Circle (Selena Fox), Daoine Coire, Dianic (Z. Budapest), Demetrian (Jennifer Reif), Druid Church of the Wise, Faerie Tradition of Y Tylwyth Teg (Welsh), Feri (founded

> by Victor Anderson [he changed the spelling from Faerie to distinguish it from other so-called Faerie Wiccas], Francesca Dubie), Gardnerian (Gardner, Valiente, many others), Georgian, Kingstone, Lothlorien (Paul Beyerl), Myjestic, Odinist (Ed Fitch), Reclaiming (Starhawk), Re-formed Congregation of the Goddess (a branch of Dianic Wicca, Jade), Seax-Wica (Raymond Buckland), Silver Crescent, and Strega (Italian, L.L. Martello, Arnold and Patricia Crowther).

Some traditions are open, hold regular public rituals, and have Websites, whereas others are so secret their members may not speak if they happen to pass on the street. Some are much concerned with lineage (it's like Apostolic succession: their high priestess must be able to trace her initiations back to the First Initiator), whereas others will accept and initiate anyone who studies for a year and a day or takes specific classes.

What I especially like about traditions is that people are creating them all the time. My friend Vajra Ma (formerly Judith Kali Evador), for example, is an ordained Dianic priestess who began working on what she called Woman Mysteries in 1990. Four years later, she established the priestesshood for her new tradition: Woman Mysteries of the Ancient Future Sisterhood. More recently, a well-known author created something called Faerie Wicca, for which she claimed archaic antecedents. Now, please understand that I am not putting any person or any "tradition" down. I think it's a good idea to create new traditions! Multiplicity is as natural as flowers and leaves and snowflakes.

Ritual Practice

The word "ritual," author Judy Grahn believes, is derived from the Sanskrit *r'tu,* which she also sees in "arithmetic," "rhythm," and "root." The most basic meaning of *r'tu,* she writes, "is menstrual, suggesting that rituals began as menstrual arts."[10] If you want a less bloody origin for what your circle does, we also know that "ritual" comes from the Latin *ritus*, "rite."

Each tradition, coven, circle, or school has its own structure for rituals (The Right Way to Do It), although minor variations are occasionally admitted. Many groups and individuals (we who practice mostly alone are called "Solitaries") rely on their Book of Shadows, which contains the outlines and scripts for the major sabbats (the eight festivals of the "wheel of the year"), full and new moon rituals, and special rituals like initiation, handfasting (marriage), wiccaning (dedication to the faith), and croning. A Book of Shadows also records traditional wisdom like spells (with expected results), recipes for incenses and oils, diagrams for arranging the altar for each ritual, and pertinent information on the use of the tools: salt, water, pentacle, sword or knife, wand, chalice, candles, incense, or whatever you choose.

It's virtually impossible to do a comprehensive survey of ritual practice, however. Some groups are closed and no visitors ever attend their rituals. Some groups hold occasional open or "outer court" rituals but keep the important ("inner court") rituals secret; we can only speculate on how their open rituals differ from their closed ones. Other groups hardly ever do the same thing twice, and sometimes a number of covens and circles will work together to stage public festivals.

Still, based on research and conversations with people who regularly do rituals, I can make a few generalizations. Seven procedural steps seem to be common:

1. *Purification.* Incense, saltwater, or visualization is used to purify attendees, the space itself, and the altar tools.

---

10. See her extraordianry book, *Blood, Bread, and Roses: How Menstruation Created the World* (Boston: Beacon Press, 1993), p. 6.

2. *Casting the circle.* The circle is cast, or closed, in sunwise (clockwise) order by calling in the powers of the four (or six) directions, the four elements, the Goddess, and (if he's welcome) the God. This is sometimes done by the priestess and her assistant, sometimes by members of the group. When the circle has been cast, it usually means that no one is permitted to come in or go out, though I've been in circles where people wander back and forth at will. Although this does major damage to the energy of the circle, some people don't seem to care.

3. *Stating the intention.* This is the purpose of the gathering, its will to be done. It can be a sabbat celebration, healing, working for world and personal peace, a prosperity ritual, or any other special occasion. I think this is the most important element of ritual. As long as you do it with intention, you can do your ritual just about any way you feel inspired to. High-Church Witches have disputed this point with me, and today I must admit that even my permissiveness has occasionally found limits. These days, I want at least a modicum of organization in my rituals.

4. *Raising energy.* The group chants, sings, or makes music by drumming and clapping, dances (spiral dance or freeform), or visualizes the rising power. The raised power, which can become volcanic, is referred to as a "cone of power." Generally the cone of power is aimed and sent out to a specific target for a specific purpose.

5. *Trance work.* The leader guides a meditation that uses the power just raised for a specific purpose.

6. *Grounding the energy.* Excess energy is returned to the earth for recycling.

7. *Opening the circle.* And we have to go back to our everyday lives. The energy is unzipped in moonwise (counterclockwise) order, all invisible powers are thanked and sent back to where they came from, and the people adjourn for refreshments and a social hour.

You're likely to find instructions on these basic steps, combined or subdivided or in a different order, in any given book on ritual. Sometimes the people "check in" first, bringing everyone else up to date on how their lives have been going and how they're presently feeling. If guests are present or the group is full of irregular attendees, checking in can include self-introductions. Sometimes the intention is stated and energy is raised before the circle is cast. People working in the Gardnerian traditions read the Charge of the Goddess and draw down the full moon — or at least its power — into the high priestess and thence into the circle. Not every ritual includes trance work or builds a cone of power, and many groups celebrate the sabbats by staging dramatic rituals and acting out the appropriate mythological story.

Although the above describes rituals for groups, solitaries often try to follow the same outlines, doing appropriate steps by themselves at their home altars.

An Eclectic Full Moon Ritual

Let's bring Green Spring Circle forward again and attend one of their full moon rituals. It's a Wednesday night at the end of March, the first full moon after the spring equinox and the weather is perfect. The circle is meeting tonight in Celeste and Maddy's back yard, which is protected by a tall ivy-covered fence and has permanent, inconspicuous altars in the four directions. Elbereth and Starling, the little girl already in her jammies, arrived first, followed shortly by Christine and R'becca, who generally carpool. Maddy has already set up a circle of lawn chairs. Now she and R'becca get out the portable altar and set it up in the middle of the circle. Although many covens place antlers on their altar to represent the Horned God, Green Spring is semi-Dianic, so there are neither antlers nor god. R'becca sets a Willendorf Mother in the center and surrounds Her with a loosely-woven wreath of early spring flowers — tulips, freesia, daffodils — and asparagus fern. She adds a bronze bell, a white pillar candle on a green clay saucer, and an abalone shell, into which she places and lights a charcoal round. Starling, who like many young children collects rocks, approaches with her newest treasure in hand. When Maddy shows her where the north is, she lays her rock at that point on the altar. Her mother adds a fist-size shell in the west, Christine lays a Ukrainian *pysanky* egg (which has been in her family for five generations) before the Goddess, and Celeste cuts a few herbs from her garden to lay among the flowers. She also lays a twig of dried sage beside the abalone shell.

Hazel arrives a bit later, frazzled and straight from her office. "Don't even ask," she growls as she fishes a cinnabar dragon out of her tote and lays it on the south side of the altar, and then goes into Celeste and Maddy's bedroom to change from her suit and pantyhose to jeans and a sweater. They are just getting ready to purify the space when Raven scurries in, lays a beaded feather on the east side of the altar, and takes her place in the circle.

Celeste wraps her silver and green shawl around her shoulders and says, "Let's get started now." Noticing that Hazel is still tense and Raven fidgety, she continues, "Everybody take a deep breath. Take another breath and feel the energy rising from our blessed Mother Earth into your feet and legs. Let it rise into your wombspace. Into your chest. Down your arms. Up into your head." She lets them breathe and feel the rising energy for a few minutes, then continues. "Now let's connect with the sky, too. Pull the energy of the stars down into your head. Let it fall down through every part of your body. Let it unite in your heart with the energy of the earth."

After a minute, Celeste nods to Elbereth, who picks up the bell and walks with her daughter around the circle behind the women. Stopping at each direction, the mother visualizes a pentacle of blue fire (while the child visualizes whatever a child might see) and rings the bell. They can hear Starling's tiny voice: "Blessed be." Right behind them,

Raven carries the abalone shell and sage to each woman and cleanses their auras with the sacred smoke. After Elbereth and Starling have rung the bell to the powers above and below, they place their implements on the grass beside the altar.

"Our intention tonight," Celeste says, "is to celebrate the spring of the year and the rebirth of light and vegetation. This month is the sixth anniversary of our circle, so let's also work for the harmony and strength of community. The moon entered Libra last night, so this is actually a good time to focus on harmony and community." Everyone nods. "And the larger community. Let's cast the circle."

Raven walks to the east side, the others turn to that direction, and they all raise their arms in the familiar chalice position. "Hail, Guardians of the Watchtowers of the East," Raven says. "Powers of Air, the Rising Sun, and the Cleansing Winds. By the Air that is Her breath — be here now."

Everyone murmurs, "Blessed be," and Raven walks behind the women to the south, where Christine is standing. As she kisses Christine on the cheek, the others turn toward the south and raise their arms again. "Hail, Guardians of the Watchtowers of the South," Christine says. "Powers of Fire, the Warmth of Noon and Cleansing Flames. By the Fire that is Her spirit — be here now."

"Blessed be."

Christine walks to the west, where Maddy is standing, and kisses her. "Hail, Guardians of the Watchtowers of the West," Maddy says. "Powers of Water, Sacred Shade of Twilight, Fresh Water and Sweeping Tides. By the Waters of Her living womb — be here now."

"Blessed be."

As the women turn toward the north, Maddy walks behind them to Hazel and kisses her. "Hail, Guardians of the Watchtowers of the North," Hazel says, her arms raised. "Powers of Earth, the Silence of Midnight, the Abundance of the Holy Earth. By the earth that is Her body — be here now."

"Blessed be."

Now the women turn again toward the center. Celeste goes to the altar and lights the pillar candle. "Great Goddess of Ten Thousand Names," she says, raising the candle. "Mother of us all, we welcome You to our circle, to our space, to our lives. It's springtime. As You are urging Your trees and flowers, Your grains and vegetables back to life, so are we being reborn to our new lives of harmony and community. Blessed Goddess, let us live and die and be reborn in the womb of Your beautiful green planet, in the passion of Your loving heart, and in the intelligence of Your creative mind."

She sets the candle on the altar and closes her eyes for a long moment. Then she continues, "Our circle is cast, the energy is sealed. Once again, we are in the place between the worlds that is no place, where all things meet in perfect love and perfect trust. Here birth and death, light and dark, joy and sorrow, and coming and going are as one."

As she walks to the chair in the north, the others sit in their chairs. "This is the first full moon of the spring," she says. "What seeds do we want to plant beneath this full moon? What do we want to grow this year?"

"Graduation," Elbereth says immediately. "And a good job so I can get a decent car and move into my own place. Maybe try living with David again."

"Then you also want good day care for the Munchkin," says Maddy. Starling is already sitting in her lap, playing with a little stuffed Blessed Bee.

"Corporate survival," says Hazel. "Productivity in my department. Peace and quiet and no more in-fighting." She grins. "And maybe I'll get to take my vacation this year!"

As everyone applauds, Christine opens her eyes. "Don's retiring in September, you know. We want to drive up to Alaska and spend some time with my son. We're also going back to St. Louis to spend time with his daughter and her family. So my seeds are for family reunion and harmony."

When someone says, "And safety on the freeways," everyone nods.

"Well," says Raven, "my seeds are already growing. DevelCo is not going to build those condos in Santiago Canyon. All the protests actually worked for once — "

" — well, you realize that a little magic helped," Maddy says.

" — Yes. And there's more seeds I want to plant: Get those off-roaders out of the canyon with their stupid bikes and SUVs. Get the equestrian center cleaned up so those horses get enough exercise. Get every dog and cat in Orange County spayed and neutered. Get every — "

"Yes," says Celeste, knowing that Raven can go on like this for hours. "Yes, good seeds. Good. Who else?"

"A good long-term temp job," says R'becca, "that's easy work so I'm not too exhausted every night and can finish illustrating Elizabeth's novel."

"Well," says Maddy, "my life's just fine, my job's just fine, my girl friend's just fine, and I feel just fine. You know what? I want to keep it that way."

Celeste smiles. "Blessed be," she says as everyone grins. "My seeds?" she continues. "I've been giving this some thought. I want to see all the covens and circles in our CoG district get together for Midsummer and do a spectacular public ritual on the beach, with lots of attendees and no interference from the beach patrol. You remember the guy who drove over our labyrinth a couple years ago? No more of that. I want to plant seeds for harmony, cooperation, and friendship among all of us neo-pagans, no matter what path or tradition we follow."

"So mote it be," says Hazel, and the others echo her. "So mote it be." "So must it be." "So shall it be."

"All right," says Celeste, "let's raise some energy to fertilize those seeds and then earth them right here so they can grow." As she and R'becca pick up their doumbeks, Maddy notices that Starling has fallen asleep. As the drumming begins, she picks up the child, cuts a door in the circle, and takes her into the house, where she will sit with her until her mother fetches her to go home.

As the drumming begins softly, a heartbeat, the women begin the MA chant. "Mmmmmmmmmmmm." Then, "Maaaaaaaaaaaaaaaaaaaaaaa." As the chant rises and overtones and harmonies sound, the drumming quickens, and soon the women are standing, hands raised to the sky. "Maaaaaaaaaaaaaaaaaaaaaaa." The women feel or see the energy moving around them. "Maaaaaaaaaaaaaaaaaaaa." Sound and energy rise higher and higher, there is a fury of drumbeats, and at last Celeste shouts, "Now! Let it go!" Sudden silence. But instead of sending their cone of power toward some target outside of themselves, the women pull it back into their circle, through their bodies, down into the earth.

Celeste touches her drum again, and a barely audible heartbeat touches the silence, heartbeats made palpable as each member of Green Spring Circle visualizes the working of her energy, the planting and fertilizing of her named seeds. Finally, there is silence, and they can all feel the energy draining down into the earth beneath them, grounding them and bringing them peace.

After several long minutes, arms and legs begin to stretch, mouths yawn, and eyes open, and Celeste knows their work has succeeded. When she judges that everyone is present, she lays her drum aside. "That was good," she says, and several of them nod. "Are we ready to open the circle?"

They get to their feet and join hands as Celeste walks to the center. She raises the pillar candle and faces each direction in turn. "Guardians of the Watchtowers of the North, all Powers of Earth, we thank you for being present in our circle tonight. Return now to your realms in peace. Hail and farewell." Using the same formula for west, south, and east, she opens the circle, concluding, "Our circle is open but never broken. May the peace and love and joy of the Goddess encircle our lives as She encircles the earth upon which we live and move and have our being. Merry meet, merry part, and merry meet again."

The members of Green Spring Circle hug each other with genuine affection, someone extinguishes the candle, and they go into the house for their potluck. They spend another hour together catching up on gossip, plans, and hopes. By ten o'clock, they're ready to go home.

Creating Ritual

Let's review what Green Spring Circle did. Remember, this wasn't a real ritual, though it could have been. One of my friends, in fact, wants to do it with her circle.

Purification. The first thing Celeste did was to tame the tensions her circle sisters brought in with them. She asked them to breathe in unison, which has an automatic calming effect. Because these women have been working together for a few years, it takes only a few silent minutes. With people who were less intimate or in a more troublesome situation, she might have begun with a longer visualization in which she guided them to see their tensions draining out through their feet and hands into the earth.

Some leaders use movement and sound to purify the space. If Green Spring were a bigger circle or they were going to do a more highly energized ritual, Celeste might have had them hold hands in the circle or dance around the altar or the perimeter. With only six, however, holding hands around the altar is too crowded and dancing around the perimeter pulls them too far apart. A wise leader looks at her group and uses common sense.

Although ceremonial magicians and covens in High-Church Witchery follow supposedly ancient formulas to purify "creatures of water and salt" with which to banish unwelcome spirits, eclectics generally find less cumbersome ways to demarcate their working space. At the Dianic Circle of Aradia, of which I'm a member, five women silently purify the space by walking in turn to each direction with elemental symbols: incense (air), a lighted candle (fire), a chalice of water, a crystal (earth), and a bell or chime (spirit). It's quite lovely. When you purify your own space, use any technique, like ringing a sweet bell, that satisfies you.

Raven used sage to clear everyone's aura. If anyone in the group is asthmatic or otherwise sensitive to smoke, however, you don't have to use sage or incense. (A chronic asthmatic myself, I always make sure I sit upwind, and I'm not shy about proclaiming that to me burning sage is air pollution.) If you want to avoid smoke, pass a half-full chalice around the circle, letting each person visualize his or her mundane worries draining into the water. Pour the water on the ground, or at least down a drain, after the ritual. You can also stroke each person's aura downward with a feather, a flower or leafy branch, a bunch of herbs, or a cotton or silk scarf. Follow the stroking with a "blessed be" or a light kiss.

Casting the Circle. The "Guardians of the Watchtowers" are also holdovers from ceremonial magic. They're sometimes referred to as the "Lords of the Watchtowers" and frequently visualized as mighty archangels bearing their fiery swords before them — hardly a pagan image. In some traditions, the priest or priestess uses the ritual sword to draw the invoking pentacles and draw the boundary of the circle to demarcate the space. If you want a less martial effect, use flowers. Or sweep around the edge of the circle with a broom. Or have attendees kiss the next person and say something like "in perfect love and perfect trust" or "the Goddess blesses you."

Some people invoke goddesses or gods, or both, when they are calling in the directions and elements. My preference is to invoke the elemental spirits (or energies) when casting the circle, but to invoke the Goddess or specific goddesses only at the center. I'll discuss the directions, elements, and invocations a bit later.

Having a different person invoke each direction both gives everyone something to do and also gives them practice. There are few things as boring in a public ritual as just standing there watching someone mumble and do mysterious things at the altar.

One person can also cast the circle from the center or walk to the directions, pointing to the direction with a wand, a feather, a flower or leafy branch, or her own hands, but she needs to speak loud enough to be heard by everyone present. You can even cast the circle sitting down and without turning to face each direction. Just be aware that these variations change the circle's energy.

"By the Air that is Her breath," "By the Fire that is Her spirit," "By the Waters of Her living womb," "By the earth that is Her body," and "We are between the worlds" show that the women in Green Spring Circle have, like everyone else, read Starhawk's *Spiral Dance*.[11]

As far as I've been able to learn, the phrase "blessed be" was created by Gardner & Co. to be a Wiccan equivalent of "amen." Although the phrase is not "traditional" in the sense that Witches have been saying it since the Middle Ages, it does have literary antecedents. Fantasizing about getting away from the hustle and bustle of eighteenth-century London, John Dryden and others wrote "Beatus ille" poems. *Beatus ille* is Latin: "blessed is he." This reminds us of the Beatitudes (Matthew 5:3–11), which begin "Blessed are the poor."

---

11. See *The Spiral Dance,* 20th anniversary edition (San Francisco: HarperSanFrancisco, 1999), chapter 4, "Creating Sacred Space."

Stating the Intention. Whether you're working alone or in a group, always be sure to say *out loud* why you're doing this ritual. You can't be focused if you're not clear about what you're focusing on. As I said before, I think this is the most important part of the ritual (though other people might say raising and manipulating the energy are more important), for when you're living and working with intention, you're practicing the presence of the Goddess.

Celeste took advantage of the spring full moon to state her intention to plant metaphorical seeds of community. She also used the movement of the moon into Libra to give it extra power. Even if, like me, you don't really speak astrologese, you can use an astrological calendar to track the celestial energies and time your own rituals to take advantage of them. Don't be a slave to astrology, however; you can do any ritual any time. When you state your intention aloud, it lets both the universe at large and your own subconscious know what you've got in mind, whatever the prevailing energies may be.

Keeping in mind the inalterable fact that what you put out comes back at least threefold, you can create a ritual with any intention, from drawing health and love into your life to banishing those who develop open lands or binding a rapist or other abuser of women and children.

Banishing and binding are very controversial topics; such spells are often called "negative" and "manipulative," and some writers say we should never, ever, ever do manipulative magic. I think that's like surrounding a criminal with White Light, the cure-all of New Thought; it's pretty but it doesn't get any work done. We can banish and we can bind, and we have a choice in how we energize our working. We can summon up the energy of righteous anger, or we can do it without anger from a position of strength. Either way, we must state aloud and with absolute clarity that what we're doing is returning negative energy to the sender. We're sending back what that abuser has himself already put out. We are, in other words, acting as a mirror, reflecting garbage rays back to their originator.

Raising Energy. There are many ways to stir up ritual energy. Alone or in a group, you can use the chants given earlier. I especially love the MA chant ("ma" being the maternal word in languages all over the world) with its rising harmonies and harmonics. When your head starts ringing, you know the chant is working. You can also chant pure vowel sounds or goddess names, and you can drum together. Repetition and rhythm are what alter your consciousness.

Dance has long been a primary means of raising energy. It is said that Shakti danced the universe into being long before anyone made a statue of Shiva as Lord of the Dance. When you're doing a solitary ritual, improvise your movement to music on tape or CD. Or shake a rattle or clap your hands. The idea is to get your energy moving, and to do that you've got to get your blood flowing. I think dance and movement are easier with a group, especially if there are experienced ritual drummers present.

With experience, you'll notice how energy changes in different kinds of rituals and with different groups. Seasonal rituals have their own energies, as do full and new moons. And while one person can raise energy that is just as strong as a group's, its quality and flow will be different. In a large public ritual, you'll soon see that the flow is more effective if people stand and hold hands while the circle is being cast, though I have also been to smaller rituals where we held hands and danced in circles. In one ritual on a beach, five or six of us danced shoulder to shoulder around a fire. (I'm amazed that we didn't all end up with scorched knees.)

Containing this raised and focused energy is the reason you cast the circle and don't let people break it. (I've noticed that animals and small children — and, strangely, photographers — seem to cause no interruptions in the flow of the energy, however much they may interrupt you.) It's like you're mixing batter for a cake. You've got to put the flour and the eggs and the other ingredients into a bowl, one that is big enough to contain all the energy, because if you don't, when you put the electric mixer into it, you'll have batter all over you, all over the counter and the cabinets, all over the walls and floor. You'll have a mess to clean up and no cake to eat. Your ritual energy is the batter of your cosmic cake.

Celeste guided the energy with both her mind and her drum. Her mind focused and guided it, and the drum beats gave it rhythm, which set up a wave pattern. The wave pattern catches all the individual energies of the individual people and brings them into resonance, or entrainment, which magnifies the power. Listen to any chant, from "No blood for oil" (popular during the 1991 Gulf War) to "Two, four, six, eight, who do we appreciate." There are regular beats. People clap or stomp or wave their banners to the rhythm and pretty soon everyone's shouting in unison. It's hard, in fact, to get out once you're entrained. You become one with the group. When you're drumming, you know you're entrained when you can't hear your own drumming anymore.

Think of the power of other rhythmic ways you raise energy. One of them results in babies.

It is useful, if you're working alone, to consciously visualize the energy and get it moving into the pattern you want. Once you get it moving, it will keep going while you concentrate on other things. If you want to, you can check back in on it from time to time. You'll see — it will still be spinning or circling. This is because the energy of a circle is also part of you, and when you get centered, you can sometimes see the "invisible" energy. If I look with my inner eyes, for example, I often see sparkling black waves pulsing back and forth. Sometimes the energy runs in patterns around me, and the green helix I suggested in the Ritual to Celebrate the Goddess in Women is typical (at least for me).

What we're feeling and seeing, of course, is the activity of our auras. But the energy we experience is not entirely intrinsic to any of us. We share it. My personal electromagnetic field, and yours too, is part of the planet's electromagnetic field. This is how I know I'm part of the Goddess, how She is immanent in me, and why I love and worship Her as I do. We're all linked in Her consciousness and to Her dancing energy.

Focusing the energy you raise is also important. Let's go back to Green Spring Circle. Hazel has a friend, Rachel, who is making a career change, from retail sales to customer support. For her new job, Rachel will have to use a computer, but she hasn't kept up with the mysteries of Word and Excel and is afraid she'll fail. So they hold a ritual for her, and because it's specifically for her benefit, they have her sit facing the altar, upon which they place an Athena, goddess of the modern world of business. During the ritual, therefore, Athena and Rachel are looking at each other, and when the circle raises energy, they focus in on Rachel to increase her self-confidence.

Try sensing your own energy, with or without music, candles, or other props. Sit quietly, close your eyes, put your body and left brain in neutral, and wait. Pay attention to the beating of your heart and the suspiration of your lungs. Pay attention to the dance and flow inside your eyelids and around your body. That's genuine energy. See if you can direct or manipulate it. Play with it. It's always there. All you have to do is pay attention to it. It isn't airy-fairy energy, either. It's entirely practical.

Trance Work. The next step is to work with the energy. Your consciousness is altered. Your will is focused, and extraneous things are set aside for the moment. You are truly in the place between the worlds, and this is the place where things happen before they manifest in our everyday consciousness and in our ordinary lives. You can guide the energy, mold it, form it, direct it. You can assert and express your will — state your intention — remembering, of course, that what you put out will come back at least threefold.

When we do trance work, we're in a hypnotic state. Our brain is running on alpha waves instead of the beta waves we need when we're at work or concentrating on something. In this alpha state, the naïve, childlike subconscious that lives in our hearts behind our walls of sophistication and cynicism is now open for unfiltered communication. It believes what we show or tell it and works simply and powerfully (if also sometimes slowly and deviously).

Celeste could have asked another member of the group to lead the visualization, and it could have taken a more concrete form. They could have visualized Tellus Mater and Ceres, Roman earth and vegetation goddesses, walking hand in hand, as they are said to do, beneath the earth, talking to plants and urging them to grow. The only limit to a visualization is your fearless active imagination, and the more outrageous an image is, the more effective it is at grabbing the energy and running with it.

Occasionally, trance work leads to divination; sometimes it results in channeling; sometimes it results in trance dancing. Just go with the flow. And keep drumming.

Grounding Energy. It is vital to ground the energy you raise. If you don't, you'll probably toss and turn all night and perhaps be jittery the next day. One good way to ground the energy that your ritual has raised is to visualize the energy draining out of your body, flowing down through furniture and floors and buildings, and soaking into the earth, where it is absorbed and recycled.

You also need to ground yourself after you leave the ritual. I often ground myself after a ritual by washing dishes or doing some other homely chore. I can do this easily because I often work at home and do many of my rituals before noon to take advantage of the rising power of the sun. Scrubbing dishes or the toilet really brings one back to earth, and remember — that's how Brother Lawrence practiced the presence of his God. You don't have to wash dishes after you get home from a ritual, but you may want to read awhile before you go to bed. If you don't ground yourself enough, you may find yourself still up in the wee hours of the morning alphabetizing your spices and CDs or rearranging the icons on your computer desktop into new and resplendent patterns.

Group hugs and refreshments — earthy foods like hummus and corn or potato chips, but not salads — and social hour also help us ground energies and prepare us to go back out into the ordinary world.

Opening the Circle. I have seen people simply "unzip" the energy and say a quick farewell to elemental spirits and other invisibles, and I've also seen people take as long to take the circle down as they took to put it up, dismissing every attendee, visible or invisible, by name.

Celeste used a simplified version of opening the circle. Instead of standing in the center, she could have walked to each direction again. There are all sorts of reasons for using a simpler closing, from being a bit unsteady on your feet to having to go to the bathroom *now*. (It happens.) Here's a practical idea for casting your circle: make it as big as your whole home so you can go to the bathroom and the kitchen without violating the boundaries.

Please keep in mind that, unlike Dr. Faustus, we haven't summoned the presence of the invisible powers so we can command them and put them to work for us. We've invited them to be present so we can all work together. (It's that tricky issue of "power over" and "power with" again.) That means that when we open the circle, we don't banish the invisibles. We thank them for being with us and for attending our ritual.

Always treat the invisibles with respect, whether they're your own mental and emotional powers, elemental spirits and devas, or angels and goddesses. Even if you can't see them, they're real, and you never quite know what they can do and when they might do it. You don't want to antagonize a god or a salamander (elemental fire spirit) or an archangel.

Some people like to say, "Go if you must or stay if you will." This gives the spirit the option. Be aware, however, that it's not safe to have elemental spirits out of control. They're notoriously mischievous. Fire elementals can bring fires, a major threat where I live, water elementals can bring floods, air elementals can bring tornadoes, earth elementals can bring earthquakes. "Hail and farewell" may be a better valediction.

"Merry meet..." is another Gardner & Co. "traditional" saying, both benediction and promise.

Unencumbered Ritual

You can make it a really big deal. You can do research in a dozen authoritative books. Build or buy a twelve-foot-tall Goddess. Set up and decorate four altars with pomp and ceremony, using the prescribed symbols for the four directions and properly sanctified altar implements. Light beeswax candles in the proper colors and anointed with the proper sacred oils. Burn specially prepared incense. Plan, write, and rehearse the scripted invocations, chants, and music. Hire a dozen drummers and flutists. Choreograph the casting of the circle with the proper pentacles drawn with sword or wand or broom. Coordinate your ritual with the phase of the moon, the movements of the planets, the time of day, the day of the week, and the season of the year. Create spectacular robes and costumes, masks and jewelry for all participants. Find a mind-blowing location with privacy, a spectacular view, growing trees, blooming flowers, and perhaps a mountain in the background. Invite two hundred of your closest friends.

It takes a lot of work to pull off a really great ritual that pulls in genuine power, and it's truly worth every bit of work you do. It can change your life.

We solitaries, however, worship alone most of the time. Our rituals are more likely to be the tiny ones that we create on the spot to celebrate a private achievement or to ask for help. We light a candle, perhaps, chant or talk to a goddess, do a brief meditation, or just sit quietly for a few minutes.

The latter is what I call *unencumbered ritual*. It's not big. It's not fancy. It doesn't necessarily follow the traditional rules and it seldom requires hardware or props. To High-Church Witches, it may not even look like a real ritual. But it works. It's repeatable and it alters your consciousness. It's very personal, and the emotional content is fully satisfying. The little rituals we've already done in this book were unencumbered rituals.

Remember — most simply defined, a ritual is a repeatable, and often repeated, working that has a specific meaning and a specific intention. The actions or the words (or both) serve to put each person participating in the ritual into an altered state of consciousness, which may be worshipful or experimental or playful. The altered state of consciousness gets us in touch with invisible powers, which may be intrinsic (our untapped imagination and unfertilized creativity) or extrinsic (goddesses, elemental spirits, or angels). It is these powers with whom we work our magic.

In its secular sense of habitual action, a ritual can be your customary morning routine and include all the little informal ceremonies you create to start and bless your day and make it work better, such as always using a special cup for your coffee or tea, arranging your workspace just so, doing little customary things before you really get to work. But it's always good to begin our day with an acknowledgment of the sacred dimension. I have a friend who faces the sunrise and drinks an intentional glass of water every morning to honor Gaia and Her watery daughter goddesses.

With ritual intention, we can make all the ordinary parts of our lives beautiful and sacred, like setting fresh flowers on the table or desk, unpacking and washing Grandma's dishes for Thanksgiving, or helping our children prepare for their first day of school or graduation (major rituals in themselves). The repeatability and predictability of our little unencumbered rituals add a bit of security to our ages of chaos. Our rituals can bring us comfort or inspiration. They can link us to the past and help us prepare for the future by making today more meaningful.

We can do our unencumbered rituals alone or with friends to celebrate the full and new moons, to empower a special project (as I did when I began work on this book), to beckon love or money into our lives, to celebrate a friend's good fortune, or to bless a new home. Any occasion is an occasion for ritual.

PART 4

Transforming Your World

Magic

When we do a ritual and work in our altered consciousness to make a change of some sort, we're making magic.[1]

Let's get clear about one point right away. Magic per se is not black or white. Magic is simply the manipulation of energy from an altered state of consciousness. The racist, sexist society we've been living in has determined that white = good and black = bad. Black magic is therefore bad and white magic is good. Gray magic is, presumably, a cop-out.

Actually, magic comes in all the colors of the rainbow and can perhaps best (but not always) be categorized by the colors associated with the chakras.[2] If you work in your garden with devas and plant energies, you are perhaps a green witch and do green magic. If you do your best work in the bedroom and your focus is Tantric, you may be doing orange magic. A priestess I know who works with children and their

---

[1]. Some people spell the word *magick* to distinguish what we do from what stage performers — who still call themselves magicians — do. I think magic-with-a-K is pretentious.

[2]. There are, of course, established systems of black and white magic. My focus, however, is on devotion, not science. For more on color magic, see Isaac Bonewits, *Real Magic* (Berkeley, Calif.: Creative Arts Book Co., 1971).

mothers is doing pink (heart) magic. Money magic is of course green and gold, and people who seek success in their career can do high-energy red magic. Me, I live in my head most of the time, writing and talking to people, so I'm probably doing blue magic. Computer folks may also be doing blue magic. I suspect, however, that any magic has a bit of the rainbow about it. People who work to blend traditions and paths of faith to build a larger community are certainly doing rainbow magic.

As I see it, magic is education. It's like going to school, where we drill in the multiplication tables, learn vocabulary and grammar, write theses and stories, train our muscles, learn teamwork, and perform scientific experiments. When we study magic and begin to do rituals, we have to drill in elemental correspondences and circle casting, learn the vocabulary and grammar of magic, learn or invent Goddess stories, exercise our intellectual and emotional muscles, work with other people and invisible powers, and perform scientific experiments (called "spells"). School is supposed to prepare us to live better in the everyday world; magic not only prepares us to live better in this world, but it also gives us access to the world where things happen before they manifest here. It's art and science combined to strengthen our intellectual and emotional powers and our will for the performance of specific tasks. The work and its results sometimes appear to be supernatural.

But you won't learn to do any knock-'em-dead tricks by reading this book, nor will you get a course of instruction in "miracles" or in developing your will so you can make people obey you. If you're looking for ego magic or recipes for spells, look elsewhere. My primary goals are worship and celebration. The magic and the power grow with the changes in your consciousness, but people probably won't even notice how powerful you're becoming. And you won't care because you're doing this not to impress anyone, but to heal yourself and to help heal the consciousness of the planet.

It disturbs me to hear words like "power" and "will" used carelessly. They're words that stand for major issues in our world, and people throw them around without definition. As I use "power," it's nearly synonymous with "energy." "Power" is a more loaded word than "energy." When I do magic, the energy I stir up is directed by my will, which is my goal or purpose, my magical intention. The energy then becomes power, or power-ful.

Power and will can be "positive" or "negative," "helpful" or "unhelpful," "good" or "bad," "valid" or "invalid." I enclose these eight words in quotation marks because they're so slippery. They lie along a continuum and slide back and forth all over it, depending on who's using them, and why. The underlying issues are "power over" other people or "power with" people, plus the question of whose will is intended. Many people say "God's will" or "Her will" when they mean "my will," and others try to overpower any group they work with.

To make it more slippery, we can put the two words together: "will power." I once studied for a year or so with a "spiritual therapeutic" school (founded by a European psychiatrist) that teaches that only God above can have will and power, or will power. People shouldn't even say "I want," because everything on earth is illusory: the only reality is God's will and power, so there's nothing real here that we can want.

Huh?

I find this kind of teaching extremely pernicious, especially to women and people of color. Like the popular admonitions to hand our power over to a higher power ("let go and let God") or to set our ego aside, this teaching assumes that the white male experience is the norm. Before they can properly engage in spiritual studies, most men do, in fact, need to set aside the power and ego in which they are wrapped as they walk about in the world. They need to stop talking and listen. But women and people of color are not part of that norm. For maybe five thousand years, we haven't been allowed to have power or egos to set aside. Until recently, we haven't had a voice to be heard. It's always been *thy will be done*.[3] You've heard it said many times: a willful girl is a naughty girl; she'll never catch a husband. A willful (fill in our own ethnic epithet) is uppity and needs to be taught a lesson.

It's time for us to find our voices and express our wills. It's time for us to regain and express our feminine and cultural powers. It's okay to say, "My will be done" and know that we mean it and that other people understand what we're saying.

But there are limits. "My will be done" should never cross the line into control and power-over. When that happens, we assume the characteristics of the people who have been our abusers, and this kind of "my will be done" inevitably leads to arrogance. For example, a priestess I once met informed me that a little after 5 P.M. on October 17, 1989, she was doing magic with a diamond ring that had been in her Bay Area family for several generations. She's bitter about how her family has treated her, diamonds are known to store and magnify great amounts of power, and — *voila!* She caused the San Francisco earthquake! I prefer to believe that she was merely trying to impress me and didn't really take responsibility for a major earthquake just because she was mad at her parents and knew something about magic.

Power issues can also lead to what are called witch wars, in which *my wand is bigger than your wand* and *I am the highest of all high priestesses*. We need to get real and get over power trips, ego games, control issues, and witch wars. We need to stop calling each other names and not respecting other ways people do things. These activities have no place in our community. How can we heal the planet while we're at war

---

3. See Carol Lee Flinders's powerful book, *At the Root of This Longing: Reconciling a Spiritual Hunger and a Feminist Thirst* (San Francisco: HarperSanFrancisco, 1999).

with each other? Instead of attacking each other, we should celebrate our diversity and gladly teach and gladly share our talents and all the colors of our magic. I used to tell my students to go to any open ritual they could find and then come back and tell us about it. We made friends and learned how to work with people who do things in ways we never thought of. Because the community is still in some ways fairly small and we love our email, gossip travels fast. But we need to cherish our community, not try to blow it apart. Acceptance of our differences will make us stronger and — who knows, stranger things have happened — we may become a positive example for the standard-brand religions to follow.

As I see it, then, developing our magical will and using magical power help us better understand ourselves and strengthen our connection with our community. Magical will and magical power also lead us back to worship of the Goddess in Her many layers and manifestations. If we lack will and power, we'll never get anywhere because we lack purpose and energy. We don't know where we're going, and someone else is probably in charge of our lives, anyway. Whether we study multiplication or magic, therefore, we should learn to express and assert ourselves, but without running over other people.

And it's not helpful to do a spell and then sit around waiting for the miracles to rain down upon us. As a friend once said while we were doing a ritual together, "Trust the Goddess and do your homework." All the better ritual books say the same thing. If we want more money, for example, we should do money rituals and burn green candles to focus our will and stir up a little personal power (though perhaps it's self-esteem we need). Then we need to get out and see what we can do to earn that money. The Goddess will meet us halfway: a job will "just happen" to be where we can find it. That's the true magic.

A Ritual of Personal Power

These words, which came to me at four o'clock one morning, reveal the context of our personal power. I hesitate, however, to use the words "personal power," because what may look like "personal power" is in fact our continuing practice of Her presence. It's not us. It is *not* ego power, it's *not* controlling people, it's *not* gamesmanship. Any power we may gain is in reality the power of the elements of the universe, the light and the dark, the Goddess herself. That is to say, the universe is a hologram and we're part of it, and *the power any of us has is simply part of that holographic power.*

Use four candles in colors you feel to be meaningful and state your intention where indicated. This intention can be fairly specific ("Help me understand this situation") or general ("I want to feel healthier today").

By the powers of the cleansing fires,
By the powers of the springing tides,
By the powers of the soaring winds,
By the powers of the growing earth,
[State your intention or affirmation]
Let my will be done. [Light first candle]

By the powers of the rising sun,
By the powers of the changing moon,
By the powers of the dancing planets,
[Repeat your intention or affirmation]
Let my will be done. [Light second candle]

By the powers of the shining light,
By the powers of the sheltering dark,
[Repeat your intention or affirmation]
Let my will be done. [Light third candle]

By the powers of the living Goddess,
[Repeat your intention or affirmation]
Let Her will be done. [Light fourth candle]

It's good to meditate or at least sit quietly in the glow of the candlelight. Where does our power lie? In what ways are we part of the holographic universe that the Goddess made for us?

Our Altar — The Earth in Miniature

When we first come to the Goddess and think what it's all about is rituals and altars, we are driven to try out every possible correspondence on our altar, which thus becomes a surfeitous expression of creativity and belief. Like the planet itself, an altar is a setting upon which we can celebrate in visual, concrete form the superabundant diversity of the manifestation of the Goddess on earth. I've never seen two altars that look alike. [4]

Here's a slightly abridged description of the altar I had in the early 1990s:

---

4. One of the best books I know on altars is *Beautiful Necessity* by Kay Turner (New York: Thames & Hudson, 1999). A small altar I had several years ago is shown in the book. See also Denise Linn, *Altars: Bringing Sacred Shrines into Your Everyday Life* (New York: Ballantine, 1999).

It's my mother's cedar chest, which I have covered with two altar cloths. Across the back of the altar, left to right: a ceramic incense holder I made myself, with a half-burned smudge stick resting in it; sacred salt I mixed myself inside a ceramic sugar bowl my brother made twenty-five years ago; my green glass, grocery store Santa Marta candle (she overcomes monsters); a 30-pound chunk of soapstone into which an owl is carved in bas relief (my major earth symbol), a chunk of wood from a friend's yard, and a carved piece of redwood from the John Muir Woods; a green figure candle that I burn for an hour every Friday for personal healing; and my gold statue of Athena. Around Athena's neck I've hung a piece of gem silica on red string and a crystal and lapis necklace (it looks kind of like a lei), and she is holding a silver pencil with a sparkly plastic star on the eraser (this is the intellectual warrior goddess's spear). In the next row are my athame; a glow-in-the-dark goddess; my egg-shaped nest of wood spheres and a quartz-crystal egg; a $3 gold-tone snake bracelet with red glass eyes; a gold, iridescent glass chalice full of beglittered wishbones and other charms; and the Priestess of Swords card from the Motherpeace Tarot. In the next row are my major candle holders (one at each side of the altar): young women's heads with faces pointing front and back, holding white "temple" beeswax candles; a glass bell with an elephant rampant (an air symbol); two Goddess feather wands (I make these); two Boji stones; a green cube candle with a gold sun face; my money jar; and a big red crayon a friend gave me, a chunk of carnelian, and a blue eversharp pencil (I use these to write rough drafts), all my fire symbols. Across the front of the altar are a small

> *wooden salad bowl full of Angel™ Cards; a symbolic knife I made from a road-killed coyote femur, an obsidian arrowhead, and a crow feather; my water symbols: a Waterford chalice (Kildare pattern) with shells and crystals in it, a sand dollar another friend gave me, and two conch shells from other friends; my magic wand (a piece of driftwood I tipped with crystal and wrapped with yarn and other things); my incense holder (a pale pink soup bowl from Pic-N-Save) and incense spoon (a condiment spoon that looks like a scallop shell).*

Whew! Sometimes it's true: too much is never enough. Back in those days, I wanted to pack every possible correspondence and symbol into my consciousness via my altar. But we all start out that way. We all want the world and everything in it.

I don't even know where most of that stuff is anymore. I suspect I've given most of it away. Today, my altars are simpler. On top of a bookcase in my bedroom, for example, is an altar to Green Tara, where She watches over photos of my family and friends. In my dining room, near the very center of my home and just around a corner from my fourteen drums, sits my home altar. At its center is a little wooden house with a figure of a woman holding a book just inside the front door. Hestia sits to one side of my little house, and on the other side, Bast watches over Her two children who live with me. A toy car is parked in front of the house, and nearby are a Blessed Bee and several rocks of which I'm quite fond.

My friend Badger Shu-Bad, a Dianic high priestess, uses the description of my old altar to give her students an example of overenthusiastic altar creation. She contrasts it to what she calls the Zen altar — rock, feather, candle, shell. She recently told me how one of her students brought to class what may be the world's best minimalist altar: a leaf. Just a leaf. It was, she said, simultaneously the altar cloth and the altar itself. It grew on a tree, which is a thing of earth, but hung suspended in air. Water nourished it, sunlight (fire) made it grow, and of course, the Goddess infused its being. As Badger asked in her email to me, "How's that for simplicity?"

All you need for your altar are simple symbols for the four elements and a candle or two and something to represent the Goddess.

All you really need is the Goddess.

The Four Elements

Any altar we create echoes Her continuing act of creation. We can make our miniature earth — our altar — more concrete by placing symbolic objects on it. These symbols call forth the four elements and the four (or six) directions.

Fire, water, air, and earth are the four traditional elements, the building blocks out of which all things, organic and inorganic, are composed. The idea of four elements, which have appeared in nearly all ancient and modern cultures around the world, was devised long before the atomic table was thought up, and elemental fire, water, air, and earth are not the same as literal physical fire, water, air, and earth. Some cultures have added other elements, like the Chinese wood and iron. In Western esoteric thought, spirit is often considered to be the fifth element, the "quintessence" and sum of them all.

Of the basic four elements, fire and air are traditionally seen as projective and masculine energy, whereas water and earth are receptive and feminine. In the tarot, the two masculine elements are represented by phallic symbols (wands for fire and swords for air) and the feminine elements are a container (cups, for water) and a pentacle or disk (earth). Gold is also considered to be symbolic of the masculine elements, and its energy is projective, whereas silver is feminine and receptive. Many people wear their gold jewelry on their stronger hand (right if you're right-handed) and silver on the weaker.

The four elements make up not only the entire physical world but also human psychology, from the four "humours" of Renaissance authors like Robert Burton and Ben Jonson to C.G. Jung's four categories and the four times four temperament types listed in today's popular Meyers-Briggs personality inventory.

Because taxonomy is a human mania, people like to put everything they can see, hear, feel, taste, smell, intuitively sense, or imagine into these four convenient pigeonholes. Here are some common correspondences.

Elemental Fire. Elemental fire rules hot places like deserts, volcanoes, and bonfires. At home, it's our hearth fires and our ovens (and maybe our microwaves). It also rules metaphorical heat: energy, creativity, will power, blood, and rising sap, as well as explosions, and eruptions. In some traditions, elemental fire rules the south, noon, and summer; I see it as dawn and spring. Fire's colors are the reds and golds; its signs of the zodiac are Aries, Leo, and Sagittarius; its elemental spirits are the salamanders; its angel is Michael (pronounced *mick-eye-el*). Fire's animals are dragons and lions, and its plants are the hot ones, like peppers, mustard, onion, and garlic, as well as red flowers. Goddesses of fire include Brigit, the hearth goddesses Hestia and Vesta, and volcano goddesses like Pele, Aetna, Fuji, and Iztaccihuatl. Fire's gods include Agni, Hephaestus, and Prometheus.

Elemental Water. Elemental water rules wet places like oceans and seas, the tides, rivers, springs, swamps, lakes, wells, and glaciers (which, since they're frozen, may also be ruled by earth), and our bath, shower, and kitchen sink. Elemental water rules the emotions and feelings, like love, sorrow, and courage, as well as intuition and sensitivity. In some traditions, elemental water rules the west, twilight, and fall; I put water in the south and give it the flooding noon and summer. Water's colors are silver and all the hues and shades of blue and green; its signs of the zodiac are Cancer, Scorpio, and Pisces; its elemental spirits are the undines; its angel is Gabriel. Water's animals are swimmers — fish, sea mammals like dolphins and seals and whales, plus sea birds. Its plants grow in the water — seaweeds, ferns, rushes, lotuses, and water lilies. Goddesses of water include the oldest ones: Isis, Tiamat, Yemaya, Mari, Atargatis, Aphrodite, Ix Chel, Miriam, and the Naiads and Nereids. Four watery gods are Poseidon and Neptune, Llyr and Osiris.

Elemental Air. Elemental air rules windy places like plains, hills, mountain peaks, and beaches above the waterline. Elemental air also rules mental activity: intellect, knowledge, theory, and intuitive and psychic work. It also rules electricity, and by extension (so to speak) our TV, computer, and appliances. In some traditions, elemental air rules the east, dawn, and the spring; I put air in the west, for dusk and fall. Air's colors are pale — white, yellow, blue-white; its signs of the zodiac are Gemini, Libra, and Aquarius; its elemental spirits are the sylphs; its angel is Raphael. Airy animals, of course, are the flying ones: birds and insects. Its plants are the ones that most often go into incense: frankincense and myrrh, also lavender, marjoram, mint, and sage, plus "air plants" (such as bromeliads and mistletoe) that grow high up in trees. Goddesses of air are the intellectual ones: Athena and the Muses, also Ninlil, Nut, Tatsuta-Hime, and Vajravaraki. Gods of air include Thoth, Enlil, and Mercury.

Elemental Earth. Elemental earth comprises the planet itself and all its earthy features: mud, mountains, caves, meadows and planted fields, forests, and groves. Rocks, crystals, metals, and bones are also ruled by elemental earth, plus earthworks like growth, sustenance, abundance, material prosperity, birth, death, and silence. At home, Earth rules the entire kitchen and all our potted plants. Nearly every tradition puts earth in the north, giving it rulership of midnight and winter. Earth's colors are greens, browns, and black; its signs of the zodiac are Taurus, Virgo, and Capricorn; its elemental spirits are the gnomes; its angel is

Auriel. Earthy animals are snakes (which live in holes in the earth) and ruminants (cows, bison, deer, and others who graze), and earth's plants are grains, grasses, and root vegetables like potatoes. Goddesses of earth include Gaia Herself, Demeter, Persephone (as Queen of the Underworld), Al-Lat, Ops, Frigg, Perchta, Hel, Tellus Mater, Nokomis, and the all-creating mother of Australia, Waramurungundji. Earthy gods are Pan and Cernunnos (the horny forest gods), Marduk, and most of the consorts who spend part of the year in the Underworld.

There's a practical reason for knowing these elemental correspondences. Everything you add to your altar reinforces your intention and beckons a specific elemental energy into your mind and heart. The more you pile on, that is, the more you reinforce both your physical senses and your imagination, the better your magic will work. It's like vitamins and other food supplements, except that I don't think you can overdose on correspondences, at least not until you run out of room in your house.

Well, maybe you can overdo it.

For unencumbered ritual, use your common sense. Simplify. What do you associate with fire? Red and orange, matches and candles, hot things. You can use a red chili pepper or a kitchen match as your symbol of elemental fire. What do you associate with water? Place a goblet of water or a shell on your altar. What do you associate with air? Place a feather or a butterfly on your altar for elemental air. What do you associate with earth? Use a quartz crystal, Indian corn or dried wheat, or a potted plant. What do you associate with spirit? Things invisible, or all things because the earth is spirit made solid. Set a Goddess image or another significant symbol in the center.

If you want to, you can use herbs for all four elements, or stones or pictures of goddesses or the four tarot aces. You can redecorate your altar for every season, for every sabbat, for every full or new moon, for every new day.

Directions of the Elements

By now you're asking, which elemental symbol goes in which direction? That can be complicated, too, since the four elements are traditionally associated with the four directions, but different traditions have different arrangements. Here are the two most common arrangements.

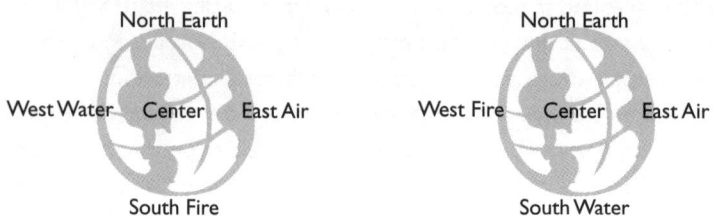

The first arrangement (on the left, above) is used by most of the modern traditions, whose roots are in ceremonial magic. It was invented in northern Europe, probably in the British Isles, and reflects the geography of the place. The North Pole is to the north, and cold = earth. The equator is to the south, and the hot climate = heat = fire. The Atlantic Ocean lies to the west, and trade winds (far to the south, to be sure) are easterly. The second arrangement (on the right, above) is based on Tantric tradition.

My own preference is a third arrangement:

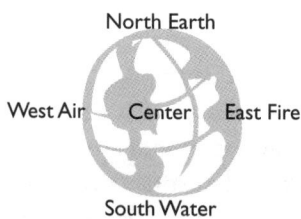

Some years ago, I noticed that in the traditional arrangement the two masculine elements are adjacent to each other, as are the two feminine elements. This looked unbalanced to me, so I rearranged the elements to alternate the energies. Later, I met a professional astrologer who had come up with the same arrangement based on the cardinal signs (Aries, Cancer, Libra, Capricorn), which are traditionally associated with the directions as shown here.

I have also interviewed other people in other traditions, including a Native American shaman, and learned that they use still other arrangements, including one that puts earth in the east.

I suggest therefore that you use whatever arrangement feels most natural and works best for you. Create your own arrangement based on the geography where you live. Do you live along the East Coast? Water is to your east. Do you live in Illinois or Mississippi or Louisiana? If the first two, significant water (the Mississippi River) lies to your west, if in Louisiana, water can be either east or south (the Gulf of Mexico). Do you live in Iowa, Missouri, or Arkansas? The Mississippi River, your significant water, is to your east. Do you live within sight of a mountain chain? That's significant earth, whatever the direction. Do you live near Mount St. Helens or Kilauea? There is your fire.

The main things to keep in mind if you create your own arrangement are to include all four elements and, when you work with other people, be sure to discuss altar arrangements beforehand so everyone is in agreement and no elemental power is invoked twice or left out.

Some people add two or three more directions: up, down, and center. Some traditions use gods and goddesses for up and down, presumably a god for up because air and fire rise and a goddess for down because water and earth are earthy. Others simply salute "the powers above" and "the powers below."

The center is the quintessential point where the four quarters meet. It's most common to put a goddess image in the center, but you can also use fresh flowers, a candle, or something that is special to you. I usually set something symbolic of my intention in the center, where it draws on the powers of the whole universe, that is, of the Goddess in all Her manifestations. The center is also where I put the candles or other things I use for the spell I'm working at the time. When I started work on this book, for example, I set up an altar, in the center of which I put a stack of computer disks. Then I brought my big, wooden Blessed Bee to sit upon them. Also on the altar were a glittery gold abundance candle in a nifty little brass cauldron, a tall gold taper, and (because three is a magical, creative number), a votive in a fancy crystal holder. You can guess what my intention was.

It seems to me that our true sacred space is the body of the Goddess and perhaps our true altar is Her heart or mind. One Christmas Eve — the night the barbarian German tribes called *Madranicht,* or Mothers Night — I was doing a 7 A.M. ritual before a cluttered altar with a friend when suddenly I heard myself say, "The earth is our altar." I think that sums it up. The earth herself is our altar and we're part of the Goddess's ritual. As long as we state our intention and with words or without them invoke Her presence, the physical arrangements don't much matter.

We should remember, also, that it's entirely possible to build a circle and an altar without any physical tools at all. We can do the whole thing in our imagination. When one of Marsha Smith's apprentices is about ready for initiation, she sits down with him or her and watches while the apprentice casts a wholly mental circle.

Altar Etiquette

When you visit someone who has an altar or go to a public ritual, *do not touch the altar. Do not pick up any magical tools or decorations without permission.* We charge our altars with the energy of our intentions and build up our own energy in our tools. When someone picks up our wand or chalice, for example, it interferes with the energy and sometimes the charge has to be done all over again. In the middle of a long-term spell, this can be very annoying; you have to begin all over again. Look at everything, therefore, and say Oooh and Aaah, but keep your hands in your pockets. When people come to visit you and look grabby, ask them firmly but politely not to touch, and explain why. If visitors won't understand, cover your altar before they arrive.

Portable Altars

We don't do all of our rituals in our own living room. You may find yourself doing a spontaneous ritual on the beach. Which way is north? You may be leading a ritual in someone else's home. You'll want to have your own tools with you.

That's why I keep my Porta-Witch Basket in the trunk of my car. For years I used a plain cardboard box, but when I found a nifty covered picnic basket in a thrift shop, I painted it black and drew glittery gold stars on it. What's in my Porta-Witch?

- A compass on a cord.
- Symbols of the elemental powers: a wooden egg with flames painted on it (fire), a shell and a four-ounce silver chalice (water), three white feathers to which I tied tiny silver bells and crystal beads (air), and a tiny silver lizard charm glued to a rock which is glued to a stick (earth).
- A little, fat Willendorf-style goddess that I made from red clay several years ago.
- Small plastic bags containing matches, tea-lights, self-igniting charcoal, sand, incenses, and oils.
- A small clay saucer to burn the incense in.
- A ritual "knife" that is really a plastic letter opener with an owl handle and a "wand" that is really a sparkly silver pencil with a star on the eraser.
- A generic altar cloth (a square yard of fabric from the remnant counter).

Another portable altar I have was made by artist Sylvia Vasquez-Lawrence. It comes in a 5 x 7 inch green plastic envelope and contains magical alphabets, numerical and color values of the alphabet, elemental and color correspondences, poppets, a selection of hand-made papers, money papers, a Goddess altar drawn by Sylvia, candles and magic matches, a candle holder, and three tiny crystals. This "Traveling Magic" kit is a handy size to keep in your car's glovebox.

If you like the idea of a portable altar, create your own and never leave home without it.

Magical Tools

You may want magical tools. Like the altar itself, your tools can be elaborate and expensive or simple and unencumbered. You really don't need any tools except your imagination, but it's fun to have things to hold in your hands.

We don't know much about prehistorical magical tools, partly because there probably wasn't much of a division between magical and "realistic" work. Every tool was a magical tool in the sense that its use added power to human labor. Hard, pointed stones and antlers were used to make other tools and carve sacred symbols into softer stone or pieces of bone. Masks were worn in rituals in Old Europe, and numerous masked figures — nearly all of them female — have been found in sites in Europe and the Mid-East. Pottery was created to contain things. Ochre, an iron oxide found mingled with clay or sand, was ground up, mixed with liquid, and painted on corpses and openings in the earth.

The so-called Witches of Christian Europe were ordinary women who had learned a few things about herbs and healing and human psychology from their grannies. Their tools were cooking pots, bowls, mortars and pestles, and kitchen knives and spoons. Because they probably couldn't afford candles, they worked by sunlight, firelight, or rushlight. They didn't have altars and probably didn't even know they were "witches." Their neighbors turned to them for the old treatments and spells when they couldn't get the help they needed from the biophobic priests and doctors of the new urban religion. Sometimes those same neighbors turned against them and turned them in.

The rituals, altars, and tools we're familiar with today, therefore, are not related to the ancient worship of the Great Goddess. They have been borrowed in modern times from ceremonial magic, which is an occult Judeo-Christian coinage and itself a great borrower from the classical pagan cultures (largely Egyptian and Hellenistic), medieval Rosicrucianism, Masonry, alchemy, the Hermetic Order of the Golden Dawn, and works by S. L. Mathers, James Frazer, and others.

Nevertheless, because so many Witches like them, let's look at the four major ceremonial tools, which are the same as the four tarot suits: swords, wands, cups, and disks (or pentacles). They correspond to the four elements: swords = air, wands = fire, cups = water, and disks = earth.

Sword. I doubt that any woman ever accused of being a witch (except maybe Joan of Arc) owned a sword. Kings, nobles, and warriors carried swords and were extremely jealous of their power. The women had kitchen knives and used them for the same chores we do today.

Instead of swords, some Witches use consecrated black-handled knives called athames to draw pentacles in the air. "Athame" is a word not found in any dictionary I own. Kelly says that Gardner got it from a story in a 1947 issue of *Weird Tales*.[5]

I also know people whose magical blades are paring knives, Swiss army knives, long quartz crystal points, and crow feathers. But you really don't need the ceremonial hardware. Instead of a ritual knife, you can use a wand to draw pentacles. You can also use a feather, a quartz point, a flower or leafy branch, a stalk of dried wheat, or your fingers.

---

5. Kelly, "Crafting the Art of Magic," pp. 43–44

Wand. The wand started out as a stick — a digging tool, the royal scepter, the conductor's baton, the shepherd's crook, the bishop's crosier, and the dowsing rod. In all cases, the wand conducts and directs energy. That is, it carries the energy in a specified direction. Because I'm a writer, the "magic wand" I use most often is my computer mouse, which I have even taken to public rituals as my altar tool.

Cup. When cups become altar tools, they're called cauldrons or chalices. Both are symbols of containment and of the ever-nourishing, ever-productive womb and breast of the Goddess.

A big cauldron (which can be your Dutch oven or any other large pot from the kitchen) is appropriate for large outdoor rituals. Fill it about a third full with sand or cat litter and burn incense (lots of it) for a really impressive effect. After you clean it out (thoroughly), you can also make soup or some other "witches brew" in it. Gourmet and occult supply stores sell small, footed iron cauldrons that can be used for various ritual purposes at home.

Being a double Cancer, I'm attracted to water symbols and own about a dozen chalices (not to mention an ocean of shells). My favorite is my Waterford "Kildare" goblet. A Tupperware cup, while not as glamorous, would work as well, however, since the idea is more important than the form. If you're sensitive to smoke or don't want to set off your smoke alarm all the time (which is what happens when incense billows up), do your purifications with water in your chalice.

Pentacle. There seems to be some confusion about "pentacle" and "pentagram." The *American Heritage Dictionary* defines "pentacle" as "a five-pointed star formed by five straight lines connecting the vertices of a pentagon and enclosing another pentagon in the completed figure. Also called 'pentagram.'" (That certainly was a lot of help, wasn't it?) So I asked around for clarification. Some people told me that the pentacle is the star itself, which becomes a pentagram when there's a circle around it. Others said that the pentagram is the geometric shape, whereas the pentacle is the tool; that is, the pentacle is the star carved on a wooden disk, painted on a plate, made into jewelry. Most of the Witches I've met simply call their piece of jewelry a pentacle.

The pentacle was drawn by medieval occultists to protect themselves from the demons they conjured up. It also occurs in nature. If you slice an apple in half horizontally, for example, you see the pentacle formed by the seeds. The pentacle can be used as the earth symbol on your altar (use that apple you just cut open) or you can hang nicely decorated ones on your walls. I have a wall full of five-pointed stars.[6]

Candles. In addition to the elemental symbols you place on your altar, you probably want at least one candle. Whether it's a nice soothing bath by candlelight, a candlelit dinner for two, or a ceremony of worship, candlelight makes any occasion special. Lighting a candle and extinguishing the electric lights signals a change of worlds; almost immediately the change of light casts you into a different mood.

Colored candles are useful to enhance your intention. Although they're more expensive than the tapers you can buy at the grocery store, beeswax candles are worth the price. They smell good and burn clean, and hand-rolled beeswax candles are often made with oils or herbs and during the appropriate astrological sign add correspondences to your magic.

You can buy expensive, elegant candelabra, symbolic holders for single candles, or use the red clay saucers that you ordinarily set your flowerpots in. This should be obvious, but I'll say it anyway: be sure your candleholders are fireproof. Keep cats, ribbons, and other flammable things away from burning candles. Never leave burning candles unattended. If you're doing a seven-day spell, snuff or pinch the flame out each time you leave your altar and relight it when you return.

---

[6]. A wonderful explication of pentacles and the number five can be found in chapter 5 of *A Beginner's Guide to Constructing the Universe: The Mathematical Archetypes of Nature, Art, and Science* by Michael S. Schneider (New York: HarperCollins, 1994).

Making Your Own Tools

I prefer to make my own tools or embellish and personalize the ones I purchase. Sometimes I tie blue and silver ribbons around the stems of goblets, and I have decorated my sword (which I got when I was initiated into an occult order) with a big bouquet of ostrich plumes, ribbons, and bells. One of my friends used to balance it on her head when she was belly dancing.

If you want to make a wand, find a reasonably straight stick about as big around as your thumb and as long as your arm from your elbow to the tip of your index finger, though shorter is all right. Glue a quartz point on the smaller end (the end that pointed away from the tree) and wrap the stick with multi-colored yarn, embroidery floss, ribbons, or all of the above. You can use any colors you like, but remember that red and orange are the fiery colors. You can also add feathers, beads, shells, bells, seed pods, or any other decorations that appeal to you. When you make your own tools and symbols, they contain your personal energy. That is what makes them truly magical.

Ritual Dress

One (hopefully humorous) definition of a Witch is "a large woman wearing colorful clothing and significant jewelry." Though High-Church Witches go robed when they're not sky-clad (naked), I think costuming is an entirely individual matter. In the privacy of your own home you can wear anything (or nothing).

To me, *anything* I wear is a costume, and symbolism and style are important to me wherever I go. Because it's useful to keep something special aside that you wear only for rituals, I also have my "crone suit," which is an elegant black Moroccan weave coat-dress with long sleeves and interesting detail in the cut. Just as lighting your candles puts you into a magical mood, so does putting on special clothing.

It's fun to dress up when you go out to public rituals. If you cannot arrange to be costumed by Cirque de Soleil, Moroccan rayon-cotton dresses make ideal ritual clothing, as do Arabian dresses, long skirts, and costumes whose elements you combine from many sources to create a properly fantastic look.

Jewelry, both at home and in public, is also important. Some people turn up at public rituals wearing every necklace they own, some wear outstanding earrings and bracelets, some wear just one special piece that they reserve for ritual work. I used to wear a dozen necklaces, but when my neck got sore, I was forced into jewelry withdrawal. Now I wear my "altar on a string." This is a long black cord strung with dangling silver symbols: a spiral, a half-inch quartz crystal, a tiny Tara, a flowering ankh, an owl, a turtle, a crescent moon, the rune *fehu*, a hand, a cauldron, and a silver cube with Bs on the faces (just in case I forget who I am).

If you play a hand drum, be sure not to wear any rings or dangly, heavy bracelets. They'll ruin the drumhead.

Some of us also wear exotic scarves, body glitter, and wonderful feathered and sequined headpieces or masks. Some of us are tattooed. Whatever you wear to a ritual, at home or in public — wear what makes you feel magical. At the same time, however, remember that people may be looking at you.

Creating an Invocation

When we invoke[7] (call in) powers, we may be addressing goddesses and gods and elemental spirits, but we're summoning our own inner power as well. All power exists both around us and inside us. Let's begin by examining invocations for extrinsic power, the transcendent powers of the universe, the invisible forces that we call goddesses, gods, devas, elemental spirits, angels, and other invisible beings.

---

7. Technically, we *invoke* powers "above" us (goddesses, devas, angels) and *evoke* those "below" (elementals). After the ritual we *dismiss* them, though I know a high priestess who says "revoke" and another who says "devoke." To me, that sounds like you're taking their credit cards away.

There are many ways to phrase an invocation. If you're in a hurry, you can try, "Powers of Earth, be here now." Or "Yo, Mama! Come here to me!" But these two invocations, while direct, are rude. And they're not magical. The more poetical an invocation is, even if it's written and spoken in prose, the more magical it becomes.

Instead of a rude summons, we can use a traditional formula, like "Guardians of the Watchtowers of the North, be present in our circle tonight and aid us in our magic." Another invocation I have used calls upon many beings: "Powers of the North, goddesses and gods of elemental earth, gnomes, angels, winds, and devas, be present in our circle." Other variations include naming specific beings. To invoke guardians of earth (in this case, a goddess, a god, an angel, a wind, and the proper elemental spirits), I might say, "Demeter and Cernunnos, Auriel and Boreas, honored Gnomes, guardians of elemental earth, we welcome you to our circle..."

Another form of invocation is not to name a specific deity but to call forth the qualities of the elemental power, what I call the power's gifts. "Powers of the North, please be present in our circle. Bring your gifts of stability, darkness, silence, and groundedness in the Goddess to help us in our magic." Refer to the correspondences given above for other gifts.

Finally, you can describe the powers in a sort of prose poem. The following comes from one of my as-yet unpublished novels:

Welcome, Powers of Earth, our Mother's body, our own beautiful bodies. Earth grounds and sustains us. Earth is rich with treasures and provides enough food for all her children. Earth is also the power of earthquakes, which destroy without discriminating between good or bad, rich or poor. And what is more powerful than an earthquake? A seed. Terrible and blessed are the powers of Earth.

A formal invocation consists of four steps:

1. Identify the goddess or god by proper name and attributes. If you want to maintain any kind of control in your ritual, it's wiser not to

invoke anyone whose name you don't know. You never know who might show up if it's an open invitation, although these days it's highly unlikely that you'll attract anyone as wicked as Mephistopheles or Asmodeus (or even Cthulhu).

And don't be afraid to invoke Found goddesses. If you look through books and lists and don't find a goddess who is specifically what you're looking for — make one up.

For example, let's suppose that, at Raven's urging, Green Spring Circle decides to do a rain ritual to counteract La Niña, which is currently drying out Southern California. Two or three of the women get together one afternoon and do some research. They decide to use rain sticks and gourds for sound and lots of blue candles, but they need a goddess of gentle rain, one who will revive the sandy soils without causing mudslides or floods. She'll be in the heritage of Tethys (mother of the Nereids) and Aphrodite, who was born in the sea, but not of Tiamat, who is too stormy. Perhaps she'll be related to the gentle Hesperides, who live and sing at the western edge of the world, for in the northern latitudes it's the westerlies that bring us the moisture-laden winds. Not finding a goddess who totally hits the spot, they decide to create one and call her Mere (pronounced *Merry*), a word related to both "mother" and "sea." One of the Virgin Mary's titles, in fact, is Stella Maris, "Star of the Sea." They envision Mere as a mermaid and ask R'becca to create a stuffed satin mermaid goddess for the altar.

Their invocation begins:

> Hear us, gentle Mere,
> goddess of the sparkling sea,
> daughter of gentle waters, nourishing springs and tides —
> Watery Mere, hear our call...

2. **Flatter and praise the goddess.** Goddesses are as vain as we are, as you'll quickly learn when you read any mythology, and surely

your grandmother taught you that we all respond more positively and quickly to sugar than to vinegar. Try this:

> Beautiful Mere,
> Crowned in pearls, robed in silver tides,
> Gentle goddess
> who brings soft rains and quenching waters
> and shines in the rainbow...

3. **Summon the deity:**

> We call you to our circle, precious Mere.
> Come into this sacred space...

4. **State your petition.** To the sounding of the rainsticks, Raven tells the goddess what specific kind of help they want:

> Gentle Mere, bringer of soft rains,
> bring your gifts to our dried-out, thirsty land —
> gentle rains, nourishing rains, soft rains
> to moisten our parched earth,
> to revive our dying plants and trees
> to let Your children drink deep.

At the end of the ritual, before you dismiss the goddess, thank her. You cannot, of course, really dismiss a goddess; she'll come or stay as she wishes, but you can tell Her your expectations:

> Blessed Mere, rain gently on us
> and then depart in peace with our thanks
> and leave your rainbow as a sign
> that when needed you will come again.

 How to Talk to a Deity

Originally, when ritual was still part of everyday life and everybody talked to the Goddess all the time, we spoke to Her in everyday words.

As time went on and priests assumed more and more power, however, exalted language and fulsome invocations arose, and pretty soon only the High Priest could speak to the God Most High. That was the state of affairs for two or three millennia.

During the European Renaissance and all the way up to the nineteenth century magical revival, it was thought that all gods spoke Hebrew by choice, and so Hebrew was the most common ritual language. Sometimes rituals were also conducted in Greek, Latin, crypto-Egyptian, quasi-Sanskrit, Enochian (the "angelic language" of the Elizabethan Dr. Dee), or all the above. If you read books on high occultism, you'll see scripts written in these esoteric tongues. Trying to pronounce them can be like trying to unscrew the inscrutable.

Fortunately, someone discovered that it can be dangerous to invoke an invisible power in a language you can neither understand nor enunciate precisely nor improvise in. As anyone who has ever studied a foreign language remembers, boners come easily and they can be very embarrassing. Worse, some powers become angry if you mispronounce their names, or you may not get who you intended to call. Like the modern Roman Catholic Church, therefore, occultists and others who do magic have generally adopted the vernacular.

But this leads us into a different verbal trap. Thanks to John Milton, John Bunyan, and James I of England (the king who authorized the 1611 Authorized Version of the Bible in English), most people seem to think that the divine eardrums resonate only to an approximation of Elizabethan English. Just eavesdrop on anyone offering a little prayer at the Rotary or Congress or a football game. It's religiobabble: "thou art," "we beseech thee," "thou saidst," and so on.

Pagans do it too. I have attended sabbats with perfectly normal Southern Californians that suddenly turn into a low-level Shakespearean road companies, complete with Renaissance Faire costumes (and weapons) and mangled language.

If you really want to essay Elizabethan English to add a fancy touch to your rituals, follow these guidelines:

- "Thou" is the singular, intimate form of "you," like the French *tu* and the German *du*. Use "thou" to address one person or deity. Use "you" for more than one. *Do not mix "thou" and "you" when referring to the same being.*

EXAMPLE: At one sabbat I attended, the circle was cast by each person anointing the next person with symbols of the four elements and saying, "Thou art god/goddess. I bless the divine in you." Wrong! It should have been "I bless the divine in *thee*." Likewise, "Oh, thou holy queen, all the world is filled with your treasures" is a no-no. It should be "... with *thy* treasures."

- For the subject of a verb, use "thou." For the object of a verb or preposition, use "thee."

EXAMPLES:

Thou art divine.
I give thee my love.
I bow to thee.
I receive this gift from thee.

- The adjective form is "thy." If the next word starts with a vowel sound, use "thine."

EXAMPLES:

Thy will be done.
Thine earth is holy.

- Use the right number (singular or plural) of verbs:

Present tense:

I am	we are
thou art	you are
he/she/it is	they are

Past tense:

I was	we were
thou wert	you were
he/she/it was	they were

Future tense:

I shall	we shall
thou shalt	you will
he/she/it will	they will

- For other verbs and poetical constructions, get out your old copy of Paradise Lost and see how Milton, arguably the finest poet of the English language, said it. Or reread your favorite Shakespearean plays or sonnets. Keep in mind, however, that no one has spoken much Elizabethan English since the early seventeenth century.

Better yet, give the Goddess and the invisible powers some credit for keeping up with the times. In public or group rituals, speak to them in standard English or whatever the mother tongue of your group is. When you're not concentrating on getting archaic subject-verb agreement straight, you can concentrate on your intention and your visualizations.

You may have noticed that the rituals in this book are written in free verse. My reason for using verse is that it is generally considered to be more elevated than prose. Verse (rhymed or unrhymed) is also easier to remember because of its patterns and repetitions, which also make the effect of the words cumulative; that is, they build to a natural climax.

Prose can be poetic, but when you choose prose, your major concern should be controlling sentence length. You need to be able to breathe regularly. Long sentences leave anyone except a trained actor breathless, and we tend to stumble on the thorns of syntax when we go on and on and on. The best way to check what you've written is to read it aloud and notice where you stumble. If your tongue trips over awkward clumps of consonants, or you gasp for breath, that's where you rewrite.

You have probably also noticed the apparent simple-mindedness of my verses. There's a good reason for simple-minded verse: it sticks in the mind and goes round and round. When you create your own verse, therefore, keep a few guidelines in mind:

- Use plain and simple words; use language the circle understands. The idea is to be direct and clear, not god-like and inscrutable.
- Use a simple rhythm. Spoken English is very nearly iambic: di-DAH, di-DAH, di-DAH. Trochaic meter reverses the iambs: DAH-di, DAH-di, DAH-di. The other two common meters are anapestic (di-di-DAH, di-di-DAH) and dactylic (DAH-di-di, DAH-di-di). Shakespeare and Milton worked wonders with these four common meters; so have Dr. Suess and Paul Simon. So can you.
- Write in short lines of two, three, or four feet. Short lines put more energy into your ritual and are easier to remember than long ones.
- If you try rhymed verse, choose a simple rhyme scheme.

AABB and ABAB are most common. Rhyming dictionaries are handy, but remember that you're not Stephen Sondheim, though by listening to his songs you can pick up interesting ideas about what can be rhymed.

The Blessed Bees

The Blessed Bees are modern Good Neighbors. Like the traditional Other Ones — Fairies, Brownies, Elves, and the like — called Good Neighbors by those who (correctly) feared to offend them, the Bees are magical beings. They respond with honey-sweet blessings large and small when we cry out for assistance. Invoke Them with these words and in your most mellifluous tones:

Twinkle, twinkle, Blessed Bees,
Grant my wish, I ask you, please.
Abundance, love, 'lectronic toys[8] —
As I will't, so mote it, Bees.

Slightly larger than the honeybees we're accustomed to, the Blessed Bees are shining golden insects with crystalline wings. They live in the Golden Hive at the summit of a glass mountain, and Melissa, Their Devoted Beekeeper-Priestess (who wears sturdy, nonskid shoes), lives nearby to serve Them. When They fly among us, the Bees carry tiny baskets, and among Their gifts to us are magical venom, pollen, propolis, beeswax, and royal jelly. Blessed Venom is used in "sting therapy" to get our attention in times of crisis, and Blessed Pollen provokes our souls to flower. Both the Blessed Bees and their relations in the mundane world have been traditionally seen as the bearers of

---

8. Insert your own line here. It doesn't have to rhyme, though it's best to try to maintain the rhythm. Bearing in mind that you might actually get what you ask for, ask for what you really want.

peace, harmony, propriety, renewal, fertility, industry, and eloquence, all of which virtues They have since ancient times modeled for humankind.[9]

In the center of the Golden Hive, surrounded by Her dancing swarm of Wonderful Worker Bees, lives the Blessed Queen, one sip of Whose intoxicating honey makes the mortal mouth golden with wisdom, both eloquent and endless. We've heard the granny tales, of course, and what child has not daydreamed of being one of those brave young heroes and heras who journeyed beyond the sun and the moon in order to seek out the Blessed Queen and serve Her for a year and a day? Some have actually gone to the Blessed Lands, and when they come back from the Land of Fairy, they're always great talkers. Some of them, alas, also write books.

Three Rituals of Blessing

I originally wrote these three rituals to open *A Woman's Book of Rituals & Celebrations*. Because people have told me over the years that they love them, I have rewritten them slightly to close this book.

A Self-Blessing

First gather twelve things or representations of things (photographs or symbols) that you believe make an accurate picture of who you truly are. These things can include your daily organizer, the keys to your 1954 Edsel, a worn silver spoon your grandmother used in her kitchen, baby clothes from your ancestors or your children, or something special you

---

9. See Joanne Elizabeth Lauck, *The Voice of the Infinite in the Small: Revisioning the Insect-Human Connection* (Mill Spring, N.C.: Swan Raven & Co., 1998), chapter 10.

collect. In addition, find a pink or bright spring-green candle, a holder (preferably black, but it can be whatever you like), and matches.

After your bath or shower, costume and adorn yourself so you look and feel like the real you, which is not necessarily the person seen by your business associates or anyone else in your public life. If you have a pet who wants to "help," invite it into your circle, but keep it away from the candle.

Sit in the middle of the floor and ask yourself, "Who am I? What makes me really Me?" Survey your collected things and begin to arrange them in a circle around you in this general order:

Behind you. Three things from your past or childhood. Things passed down to you. Things you've always loved.

Before you. Three things new to your life. Recent acquisitions, evidence of new interests. Things that indicate where you're going.

To your left. Three "left-brain" things. Things associated with words and numbers, logical thought, order, business, rational and intellectual thought.

To your right. Three "right-brain" things. Things associated with art, creativity, comfort and luxury, feelings, the religious or spiritual part of your life, beauty, and nature.

If you can, distribute these objects evenly throughout the four quarters in this circle of your life. If you can't, however, that's all right. Very few people are symmetrical. Put each thing in the quarter where it belongs, even if your circle ends up lop-sided. Light the pink or green candle and set it before you so it becomes the thirteenth element of the circle of your life.

Close your eyes, take several deep, easy breaths, and visualize or imagine the pink or green light from the candle surrounding you, filling your space, illuminating your life circle. Breathe in this light so it also fills your body. Feel the peace and love, the freshness and joy of this light in your life. Feel the energy of the things around you rising and joining the candlelight. Feel this energy flowing into every cell in your body. You can open your eyes and read the following blessing or tape it beforehand and listen to it. You can also use it as a model to write your own words of blessing.

> I bless myself
> and these things that make the circle of my life.
> I bless myself
> and my past.
> For in blessing my past
> and these things that I bring from ages past
> I become who I am now.
> Good or bad, cheerful or painful, my past is a blessing,
> for it has formed me
> shaped me
> held me
> released me
> thrust me into the present.
>
> I bless myself
> and these things to my left and right.
> I bless myself and who I am today.
> For in blessing both my intellect and my emotions
> and these things I gather into the life I live now
> I recognize who I am now.
> Left and right
> rational and spiritual
> words and images
> austerity and comfort —
> I bring divisions together.

My present blesses me
for it is how I am in the world.
It pulls me out of the past
and thrusts me into the future.

I bless myself
and the things that point to what is to come.
I bless myself
and my uncertainties, my potentialities, my future.
For in blessing what is new in my life
I move toward what I can be:
unknown but shown
unpredictable but mapped
potential to be fulfilled.
My future is waiting for me.
I bless and give thanks for every day of my life.

A Blessing for Our Foremothers

First get out the old family photo albums and family souvenirs. Select photos of your mother, your aunts, your grandmothers, great-aunts, great-grandmothers, as many female ancestors as you can find. If you can't find photos, select artifacts — an antique silver spoon, a cameo broach, a crumpled ribbon, a hankie, a quilt. Lacking photos or objects, you can write their names on small pieces of white or lavender paper (parchment is best), and if you don't know their names, write titles like "father's great-great-grandmother." If your family doesn't save things, write something like "all my female relatives, living and dead" or "my foremothers, back to the beginning of time."

Line these photos or mementos up in front of you either on a table or simply on the floor and, for a few minutes, think about what they represent. Can you visualize this long line of female relatives? How far back does this line reach? What countries did they live in? How did they live their lives?

Next, add to your collection photos of women you admire but are pretty sure you're not related to: Eleanor Roosevelt or Eleanor of Aquitaine, Cleopatra or Jinga Mbandi, Amelia Earhart or Marie Curie, Golda Meir or Indira Gandhi. Cut photos out of magazines or, if you don't want to mutilate a book or magazine, make a photocopy or hold the book open so that the photo you have chosen is visible. Contemplate your collection of heras. These are some of the women you will be blessing. You will also be attracting their powers to yourself.

Lay your collection of photos and mementos in one or more circles (or a spiral) around the candles. Let the photos overlap. Neatness doesn't count here. Inclusiveness does.

Light two candles, lavender and red. Lavender is a traditional color of the Goddess and red is traditionally associated with the Mother aspect of the ancient Triple Goddess. Now close your eyes and take a few deep, easy breaths. Visualize your mother, your grandmothers, your aunts... all the women of power in this long line circling your candles. See yourself in your place in this line. Feel their power, their love, their labor, their successes. Feel their energy.

Sit quietly and think of the old family stories. Think about books you've read that have had active female protagonists, movies about women, myths of goddesses and heras. Remember the stories of strong, interesting women.

You can open your eyes and read the following blessing or tape it beforehand and listen to it. You can also use it as a model to write your own words of blessing.

In the presence of the Most Holy Ones —
the Mothers of my body
the Grandmothers of my soul —
I give thanks.
I give thanks that I live
through their energy
through their love
through their labor.

As a daughter [son] of their wombs and works,
I return their blessings:
I bless my mother/stepmother, [name].
I bless my grandmothers, [names].
I bless all the women of my family line,
those whose names I know
and those whose names have been forgotten.
I bless the women of prehistory —
the strong, the unnamed, the forgotten.

I bless the memories of the unknown women
who tamed fire
who created agriculture
who domesticated animals
who invented crafts and sciences.
Their works have been forgotten
or co-opted by men.
May we remember the true creators, our foremothers.

I bless the women of historical times,
the queens, warriors, judges, and healers —
victims of exploitation
victims of suppression
victims of invading cultures.
Never again will women be murdered.
Never again.
I bless their souls
I bless their ashes.
Mothers and grandmothers, foremothers and foresisters —
I, your descendant, bless your works.
I, your child, bless your memory.
I, your daughter [son], give thanks for your blessed life.

A Blessing for Our Children

First find a photo of the earth taken from outer space, one of those famous photos of our beautiful blue planet. They've been published in many magazines, and stickers are also available, so it should be easy to find one. Place this photo on a table between two white candles.

If you have children, grandchildren, nieces, or nephews, get photos of them (recent or old) and lay these photos in a circle around the picture of the earth. Find photos of other children, kids from all the countries of the world, all doing their kid things or assuming adult responsibilities. Make a circle with these photos around the two white candles, your own kids, and the earth.

Light your candles. Close your eyes and take several deep, easy breaths. Feel the blessing energy from the candles, the cleansing energy of the white light. Feel the energy of all these children, both at their most raucous and adventuresome play and in repose, study, or sleep.

Spend some time thinking about the energy and wonder children bring to our lives — seeing ordinary things through their new eyes, for example, or living each day as a new adventure. Think about what children bring to the world, what their potential can bring to the world. Think about the state of the world: progressive and repressive politics, famine and hunger, wars and threats of war, the "childization" of poverty. Think about the state of the planet: polluted air and water, burning forests, suffering and dying birds, animals, and people. Is this the kind of place you want your kids and their kids to live in?

Read the following blessing or tape it beforehand and listen to it or use it as a model to make up your own words.

> Children of the living earth —
> I bless you.
> Children of so many living cultures —
> I bless your ways.
> Children of our hopes and lives —
> I bless your dreams.
>
> I bless your games, your work, your learning,
> I bless your ambitions and your reaching forward.

But our earth is imperfect —
our land is wounded,
our air and water are wounded,
and our children are wounded.
But people are at war —
nation against nation,
tribe against tribe,
and our children are wounded.
Children of genocide and ethnic cleansing,
I bless you.
May you live in peace.
Children of poverty,
I bless you.

May you always have enough to eat and drink.
Children of our wounded, stumbling planet,
I bless you.
And I promise you:
I will act to ensure you a future
I will act to restore your home.
Precious children, bright blessings.

Appendices

Appendix A: Revisionist History

We're still getting revisionist history or wishful thinking or both in many of the books now available on Witchcraft, Wicca, and neo-paganism. Ten years ago, for example, I still believed that the Inquisition had burned nine million witches during the Witch Hunt of the Middle Ages. I have since learned better.

To recapitulate the current, unromanticized scholarship very briefly: (1) The Witch Hunt was really a war against women. (2) It occurred not during the "dark ages" but during the Renaissance and the Age of Enlightenment, at the same time the famous humanists were translating classical literature and creating great art and architecture. (3) Most of the accused considered themselves to be good Christians. They did some healing and made a few charms, but they seldom attempted any serious magic. (4) Most of the persecutions occurred in the lands where religious wars between Catholics and Protestants were the bloodiest and religious bigotry the most virulent. (5) Most of the executions were carried out by civil authorities. (6) The population in Europe was simply not adequate for nine million people to have been killed. A more realistic number may be 15,000 executions.[1]

That said, I believe that *one* murder of *one* woman is *too many*.

Another of our favorite myths tells of the Indo-Europeans, or Kurgans, galloping out of the Russian steppes and into Old Europe, where they totally obliterated the civilization of the Goddess. The Indo-Europeans are our favorite villains. But they're our ancestors, too, and we need to remember that even our beloved Celts were Indo-European. Nevertheless, we like to think that all good things were matrifocal and matrilocal until those equestrian bastards arrived and forced their dominator society on great-grandmama and great-grandpapa.

---

1. See Jenny Gibbons, "The Great European Witch Hunt," in *PanGaia* (Autumn 1999), pp. 25–34. Also worth reading is Leonard Shlain, *The Alphabet Versus the Goddess: The Conflict Between Word and Image* (New York: Viking Penguin, 1998).

Appendix A: Revisionist History

The only author I know of who explains what most likely happened around 4500–4000 B.C.E. is Riane Eisler. Relying on up-to-date scholarship, Eisler[2] says that the invasions were "mass population movements" that included women and children and were triggered by dramatic climate changes in central Asia, or "Saharasia." Farming never was possible in this area, and the further depletion of the environment led to pastoralism. Life was so hard that people came to associate life with pain; eventually, inflicting pain became a way of life. With further changes in the climate, the pastoralist society was forced to move into new lands just to survive. I am vastly oversimplifying a scholarly chapter of Eisler's *Sacred Pleasure;* please read it for yourself for the supporting evidence.

So why our preference for revisionist history? One reason is that "real" history is just too bloody, too martial, too male-dominated. Another is that the history of the standard-brand religions is ... well, ditto. What did the history we learned in high school focus on? Wars and kings. What did you memorize in confirmation class? The conjectured words of holy men who were jealous of other gods (and who demonized the goddesses) and who excommunicated and declared war against heretics and apostates. It is a fact that Western Civilization has been dominated by men. In classical Greece — where democracy was invented — for example, women were confined to the home. They never went out. From ancient times until recently, mothers and daughters were the property of the fathers (which is why daddy still gives the bride away). Until recently, religious women in the standard-brand religions have had to content themselves with being "handmaidens" of the Lord and servants of the bishops and the priests and the preachers. These are, of course, vast generalizations; for detailed documentation,

---

2. Riane Eisler, *Sacred Pleasure: Sex, Myth, and the Politics of the Body* (San Francisco: HarperSanFrancisco, 1996), chapter 5

read books by authors like Mary Daly, Patricia Lynn Reilly, and Uta Ranke-Heinemann.[3]

What I'm asking you do to is *think for yourself*. Don't accept what you read just because someone published it. Some publishers don't believe in fact checking or fail to recognize sloppy scholarship and plagiarism, so a great deal of imaginative literature gets published as nonfiction, and naïve readers swallow it whole. I believe that it's time for Witches to grow up and leave the old tales behind. Mythology and folk tales can be both entertaining and instructive, but let's recognize them for what they are. Like *The Mists of Avalon,* they may present a kind of spiritual history but they are not factual history.

What we need are intellectual rigor and common sense. If we are to thrive as a valid, legitimate religion in the modern world, we need to know our history. It's true that there was a civilization of the Goddess in Neolithic Europe. From that time until our own, it's true that the goddesses have been diminished into fractions of their former selves. We are not so much re-creating an archaic religion as inventing a new religion. But let us work to create a kinder, more tolerant, more diverse religion than the religions from which we have fled.

So can it be. So must it be. So let it be.

---

3. Mary Daly, *Gyn/Ecology: The Metaethics of Radical Feminism* (Boston: Beacon Press, 1978). Daly is a very angry woman, and this book can be a real eye-opener. Patricia Lynn Reilly's *A God Who Looks Like Me: Discovering a Woman-Affirming Spirituality* (New York: Ballantine, 1995) is anodyne to confirmation class. Uta Ranke-Heinemann, *Eunuchs for the Kingdom of Heaven: Women, Sexuality, and the Catholic Church,* translated by Peter Heinegg (New York: Doubleday, 1990), was fired from her professorship at a Catholic university.

Appendix B: Goddess 101 Basic Library

Adler, Margot. *Drawing Down the Moon: Witches, Druids, Goddess-Worshippers, and Other Pagans in America Today.* Rev. ed. Boston: Beacon Press, 1986.

Anderson, William. *Green Man: The Archetype of Our Oneness with the Earth.* New York: HarperCollins, 1990.

Ardinger, Barbara. *Goddess Meditations.* St. Paul, Minn.: Llewellyn, 1998.

Bernstein, Frances. *Classical Living: Reconnecting with the Rituals of Ancient Rome: Myths, Gods, Goddesses, Celebrations, and Rites for Every Month of the Year.* San Francisco: HarperSanFrancisco, 2000.

Budapest, Z. *Summoning the Fates: A Woman's Guide to Destiny.* New York: Harmony Books, 1998.

———. *The Grandmother of Time: A Women's Book of Celebrations, Spells, and Sacred Objects for Every Month of the Year.* New York: Harper & Row, 1989.

Cunningham, Elizabeth. *The Return to the Goddess: A Divine Comedy.* Barrytown, N.Y.: Station Hill Press, 1992.

Davis, Elizabeth and Carol Leonard. *The Women's Wheel of Life: Thirteen Archetypes of Woman at Her Fullest Power.* New York: Viking Arkana, 1996.

Dexter, Miriam Robbins. *Whence the Goddesses: A Sourcebook.* New York: Pergamon Press, Athene Series, 1990.

Eisler, Riane. *The Chalice & the Blade: Our History, Our Future.* New York: Harper & Row, 1987.

Eller, Cynthia. *Living in the Lap of the Goddess: The Feminist Spirituality Movement in America.* New York: Crossroad Publishing, 1993.

Gadon, Elinor W. *The Once & Future Goddess: A Sweeping Visual Chronicle of the Sacred Female and Her Reemergence in the Cultural Mythology of Our Time.* San Francisco: HarperSanFrancisco, 1989.

Gimbutas, Marija. *The Living Goddesses.* Edited and supplemented by Miriam Robbins Dexter. Berkeley, Calif.: University of California Press, 1999.

Johnson, Cait and Maura D. Shaw. *Celebrating the Great Mother: A Handbook of Earth-Honoring Activities for Parents and Children.* Rochester, Vt.: Destiny Books, 1995.

Lauck, Joanne Elizabeth. *The Voice of the Infinite in the Small: Revisioning the Insect-Human Connection.* Mill Spring, N.C.: Swan-Raven & Co., 1998.

Monaghan, Patricia. *O Mother Sun! A New View of the Cosmic Feminine.* Freedom, Calif.: Crossing Press, 1994.

———. *The New Book of Goddesses & Heroines.* St. Paul, MN: Llewellyn, 1997.

Muten, Burleigh, ed. *Return to the Great Goddess.* Boston: Shambhala, 1994. Her datebooks are published every year.

Noble, Vicki. *Shakti Woman: Feeling Our Fire, Healing Our World. The New Female Shamanism.* San Francisco: HarperSanFrancisco, 1991.

Pollack, Rachel. *The Body of the Goddess: Sacred Wisdom in Myth, Landscape and Culture.* Boston: Element Books, 1997.

Redmond, Layne. *When the Drummers Were Women: A Spiritual History of Rhythm.* New York: Random House/Three Rivers Press, 1997.

Reif, Jennifer. *Mysteries of Demeter: Rebirth of the Pagan Way.* York Beach, ME: Samuel Weiser, Inc. 1999.

Reilly, Patricia Lynn. *A God Who Looks Like Me: Discovering a Woman-Affirming Spirituality.* New York: Ballantine Books, 1995.

Roderick, Timothy. *Dark Moon Mysteries: Wisdom, Power and Magic of the Shadow World.* St. Paul, Minn.: Llewellyn, 1996.

Shlain, Leonard. *The Alphabet Versus the Goddess: The Conflict Between Word and Image.* New York: Viking Penguin, 1998.

Starhawk. *The Spiral Dance: A Rebirth of the Ancient Religion of the Goddess.* 20th anniversary edition. San Francisco: HarperSanFrancisco, 1999.

———. *Truth or Dare: Encounters with Power, Authority, and Mystery.* New York: Harper & Row, 1987.

Telesco, Patricia. *Magick Made Easy: Charms, Spells, Potions, & Power.* San Francisco: HarperSanFrancisco, 1999.

Turner, Kay. *Beautiful Necessity: The Art and Meaning of Women's Altars.* New York: Thames & Hudson, 1999.

Valiente, Doreen. *An ABC of Witchcraft: Past and Present.* Custer, Wash.: Phoenix Publishing, 1973.

Acknowledgments

Because writing is essentially a solitary pursuit, I depend on my friends for care, feedback, and vestiges of sanity. As always, therefore, I give thanks for the presence (in person or via email) of Sandra Caton, Elizabeth Cunningham, Miriam Robbins Dexter (my Latin consultant), Ed Fitch, Glynna and Ailin Goff, Rayna Hamre, Beth Johnson, Patricia Kelly, Betty and Terry Kennard, Sandra and Ron Lange, Leticia Layson, Patti Leviton, Burleigh Mutén, Valerie Meyer, Patricia Monaghan, Anne Niven, Maria Piscopo, Sandra Richmond and Darcelle Foster, Tim Roderick, Nancy Scott, Judy Semler, Badger Shu-Bad and Harvest Brown, Arlene Solomon, Michael Van Ark and Angelo Circo, Suzan Walter, Susan Webster, Kelly Willis, and Kathleen Zundell. Special thanks to Theo Clark for letting me use her printer when I wore mine out. For producing a smashing book and not letting me embarass myself in public, thanks go to Mary Ann Casler, Susan Gilmer, Georgia Hughes, Mike Mollett, Tona Pearce Myers, and Kathy Warinner.

I am enormously grateful for *community*: Z. Budapest, the Circle of Aradia, the Orange County Local Council of Covenant of the Goddess, and the uppity, splendiferous women of the Crone Salon.

When I began writing the first edition of *Rituals & Celebrations*, I repeatedly called on my friends Marsha Smith and Clarissa Ingebetsen for both information and support. Marsha, whom I call The High Priestess Who Knows All and Tells Some, invariably supplies information I can't find in books about obscure traditions and occult practices. She also passes along some really good gossip.

The night a few years ago when my Maine Coon cat, Heisenberg, snuck out an open door and didn't come home, I immediately phoned Clarissa. She went into her secret magical place and found him. "Kitty," she said, "you'd better get home. Right now." She and I were on the phone the next night when Heisenberg sailed back over the fence and strolled into the house. Even Clarissa doesn't know precisely where he'd been, but there's no question that she'd spoken firmly to him.

A decade later, my friends and I have been through divorce and new love, through sickness and healing, and through moves of job and home, through evolution in our thinking. Marsha, you're still a source of knowledge and wisdom. Clarissa, your magic is still awesome.

I never tire of saying that the Goddess manifests *in us, through us,* and *as us*. One way we practice the presence of the Goddess, therefore, is to see Her in our friends. As friends, we practice Her presence in kindness, in honesty, in caring, in keeping in touch. As community nourishing and supporting each other, we manifest Her presence on a thirsty planet.

About the Author

A scholar-priestess, Barbara Ardinger lives in Southern California with her two cats, Schroedinger (an elderly, cranky Calico) and Heisenberg (a large, helpful Maine Coon Silver Cream). Also occupying (well, filling up) her house are multitudes of books, goddesses, witches, drums, and Blessed Bees.

You can email Barbara at barbara@visionaryfiction.com.

New World Library
publishes books and cassettes that inspire and challenge us
to improve the quality of our lives and the world.

Our books and tapes are available
in bookstores everywhere.
For a free catalog of our complete library
of fine books and tapes, contact:

New World Library
14 Pamaron Way
Novato, CA 94949

Phone: (415) 884-2100
Fax: (415) 884-2199
Or call toll free (800) 972-6657
Catalog request: Ext. 50
Ordering: Ext. 52

E-mail: escort@nwlib.com
Web site: www.newworldlibrary.com